OLD BONES, YOUNG SPIRIT

OLD BONES, YOUNG SPIRIT

An Experienced Cyclist's 15-Day Adventure Around Lake Michigan

JOHN McSHEA

MISSION POINT PRESS

Readers are encouraged to go to MissionPointPress.com to contact the author or to find information on how to buy this book in bulk at a discounted rate.

 MISSION POINT PRESS

Published by Mission Point Press
2554 Chandler Rd.
Traverse City, MI 49696
(231) 421-9513
MissionPointPress.com

ISBN: 978-1-961302-67-9
Library of Congress Control Number: 2024910112

Printed in the United States of America

To Jeanine, my true support team.

To Johnny and Ginny, my two little angels: may the skies be always blue
and the wind always at your back.

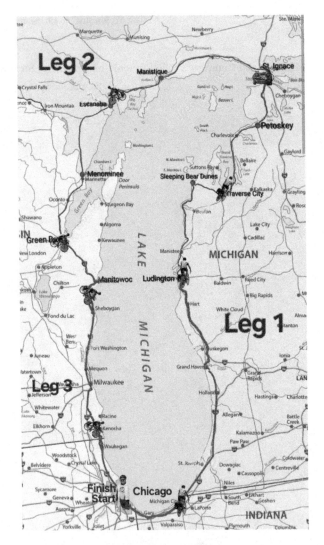

Graphic by Kristin McShea

Life should NOT be a journey to the grave with the intention of arriving safely in an attractive and well-preserved body, but rather to skid in sideways, chocolate in one hand, glass of wine in the other, body thoroughly used up, totally worn out and screaming "WOO HOO what a ride!

—Hunter S. Thompson
Author, "Hell's Angels"

Once we believe in ourselves, we can risk curiosity, wonder, spontaneous delight or any experience that reveals the human spirit.

—E. E. Cummings

CONTENTS

CONTENTS

OLD BONES, YOUNG SPIRIT

Little Johnny and me after a training ride

INTRODUCTION

If you asked my family, they would probably describe me as a bit antsy. I need to be doing something, going somewhere, seeing something interesting, trying something new. That is why cycling is such a great hobby for me. I especially like riding across new terrain and seeing something for the first time. If I can meet new people at the same time, that is all the better.

I started cycling on a serious basis around the age of 30 to get back in shape. My late 20s were busy years career-wise, family-wise and socially, and I was starting to look the part. I am now more than twice that age. I still love to ride, which has led to many great trips, long and short, all over the United States. If I had to sum up where I am now, it would be "old bones, young spirit."

Bored and antsy, I knew my friends' *Lobsterfest* party in Michigan City, Indiana, was coming up over the Labor Day weekend and a light bulb went on with the idea of riding the 75 miles around the southern rim of Lake Michigan to their place, and then to just keep going, up the western shore of Michigan.

I have always been more of a "Why not?" kind of guy than a "Why?" guy. Planning the trip was easy, but it included a lot of gray zones. I had done many long rides all around the United States, so I had a certain comfort as to what was in store. Yet this would be my longest ever, in terms of time and distance. I would be going counterclockwise around Lake Michigan, potentially more than 1,100 miles in total, and I'd be winging it for the most part.

I had cycling-route guidance via Google Maps and Garmin, but I would find that those tools would end up having their good days and their bad. They knew where they wanted me to go, but I found that the suggested route was not always the most up-to-date or ideal, given my riding style, bike setup, the road's conditions and the day's conditions.

I generally knew where I wanted to go with a couple of question marks. Those question marks were primarily focused on far northern Michigan and the Upper Peninsula. If things did not work out, I knew I could always toss my bike into the lake, rent a car, phone a friend or hop on the S.S. Badger ferry across the lake.

If all was okay, my plan was to ride up the eastern shore of Lake Michigan, divert to Sleeping Bear Dunes National Lakeshore and northern Michigan, go across the Mackinac Bridge into the Upper Peninsula of Michigan, through the UP, and then down the western shore of the lake in Wisconsin, ending up back to Chicago. No problem. Easy-peasy.

The route across the UP was one of my unknowns as I had received differing opinions as to what would be ridable, and what would not. This would take care of itself. The biggest uncertainties would, of course, include weather, bike reliability and whether my body would hold up. The weather is the weather, especially in the Midwest. One needed to plan for all possibilities.

My bike was a classic carbon-fiber road bike bought when Lance Armstrong and the U.S. Postal team were in their glory and prior to most performance-enhancement discussions. It had some age. It had also seen thousands of miles, but I had always maintained it well, and upgraded and tuned up when necessary, so I was comfortable there.

Unlike weather, age is not age. Everyone is unique, and we are always evolving, for the good and bad. At this point in my life, I felt strong and really did not have anything evident that could throw a wrench into things, so that was a "go."

I did not do this ride to write a book—just the contrary. I did the ride to ride and see a unique part of America. Toward the end of training, I added a good cause to the endeavor, the Danny Did Foundation, which raises money for families needing seizure monitors at night for kids afflicted with epilepsy. Danny Did was a cause close to my family, a cause doing tremendous work, and, with the help of Danny Did's leadership, was easy to put together for this ride.

Due to this charity, and my daily blog to donors and friends describing the crazy daily events, the wacky places I stayed and the people I met, I decided to write a book. I hope you find it as entertaining as it was for me to experience it. The trip ended up being 1,150 miles in total over 15 days. I was shooting for 14, but as you will read, things came up.

The book is broken down in chronological order as I rode around the lake counterclockwise, starting and finishing in Chicago. Each chapter highlights a day of the ride.

As a cyclist, this route had everything you would want. The variety included urban riding, amazing bike paths that seemed to go on forever, small county roads and state highways with decent shoulders. I found both Michigan and Wisconsin to be extremely bike-friendly with just a few exceptions.

I figure my story has a little something for most people. If you are like me and love all things Lake Michigan and the Great Lakes, there is most definitely a lot of that. The same goes for fans of the states of Michigan and Wisconsin as this is where I spent 90 percent of my time over the 15 days. If you love cycling, and adventure cycling, you will most definitely enjoy this story. If you like entertaining history and geography, read on. If you appreciate any time someone over the age of 50 can get off the couch and do something productive, this might be for you. Here is my story.

Lake Michigan Sunrise

PREFACE

Somewhere in the Middle of the UP

The rain was intensifying. It started as a mist, then an annoying mist, trickling down into the areas not meant to be wet, then stinging pellets. To my left—only 6 to 8 feet to my left—huge 12-ton semis filled with logs, FedEx packages and everything else Amazon deemed revenue-producing, Ford F150s and Chevy Silverados and other vehicles hummed by at 70 mph, bringing their spray wash with them. I was unmoved. I was "in the zone." I was on a bike. I was on a road bike, separated by only a few feet on the shoulder and that annoying rumble strip that snaps those drivers back to reality.

My bike was not just any bike. It was a 20-year-old, carbon-fiber-frame Trek carrying everything I possibly needed for this ride. That included skinny tires, aero bars, Garmin for GPS, waterproof phone case, tool case, two water bottles and two panniers on the back. The panniers were packed tightly with cycling clothes, two sets of shorts and T-shirts for after riding, protective rain gear, energy bars and other food, more tools, and my all-purpose flip flops. This was day nine of my journey around Lake Michigan. I was crossing, east-to-west, the Upper Peninsula of Michigan on Highway 2.

If looking at a map, the east-to-west route looks relatively straight. In real time, there are endless curves and undulating, rolling hills with long stretches of remoteness. The only reminders that humankind had stepped foot in the Upper Peninsula were the never-ending black asphalt I was riding on, the steady stream of traffic randomly attacking me from behind and the countless billboards. Besides those signs of modernity, a lot of what I saw appeared unchanged from the days of those 17th century French missionaries as they ran their canoes ashore in the hope of spreading the Word to the less enlightened.

Thoughts of "why am I doing this stupid ride?" and other negative missives were dismissed as quickly as they came. I had no time for that noise. I still felt okay, physically. The bike was holding its own. My rain-soaked garb would dry. It was not freezing yet. This ride was bigger than just me. I had friends and family looking forward to my daily blogs. Some had even commented that my reports from the day before were the first thing they grabbed in the morning. Plus, I had raised a considerable sum for Danny Did. Just shut up and ride.

I flashed back to the start, even before the start, sitting in my vintage Greystone in Chicago, as my plan quickly came together. Now nine days in, I flashed to Jerry Garcia and I thought, *"What a Long Strange Trip It's Been* so far." I knew there was more fun to come, and I could not wait.

BEFORE DAY ONE

"Where Are You Going?"

"What are you doing?" I somewhat heard, but not really, as Jeanine asked the second time.

"What?" I responded, and then offered, "oh, I am going for a bike ride."

"What's with all the stuff?" Jeanine followed up, and then added, eyes narrowing, "*Where* are you going?"

I finally released the balloon, with a smile in my voice, saying, "I'm going around the lake."

That is how it started. The Pandemic had come and stayed, the local and national news had become unwatchable, my sports teams had become even more unwatchable, and I was itching to do something, anything, positive. Jeanine was used to these slightly out-there endeavors. There had been previous bike trips through Minnesota, the Pacific Northwest and New England. Climbing trips out west and South America. In fact, on one trip the whole family went on a four-day camping and hiking excursion up and into Machu Picchu, the 15th century "lost city of the Incas." It was challenging the whole way but filled with lifelong memories. The dinner tent, high in the Andes, with the famed star constellation Southern Cross, from Crosby Stills & Nash fame, rising just overhead, was most memorable, as was the last-day hike into Machu Picchu. I was looking for another adventure.

Offering the details of my plan to Jeanine, a plan obviously containing massive Costa Rican-sized potholes, I proceeded to describe my vision. I would head out just before Labor Day, hit our friends'

Lobsterfest party in Michigan City, Indiana, shoot up the Michigan shore, and then continue north into either northern Michigan and the Upper Peninsula, or abandon my dream and take the S.S. Badger ferry over to Wisconsin and head back to Chicago.

"People are back at work, the weather is a bit cooler, and fall is beautiful in Michigan," I added. It made sense to me.

"Where are you going to stay? Are you going to camp?" Jeanine asked, after a too-long silence.

"I'm too old to camp," I replied. "I'm going to stay in motels, you know, pure Americana."

With Jeanine's one-word reply "Yuck!" I knew I had her tacit approval.

The trip was on!

With Labor Day approaching, I knew I had work to do. I needed new panniers to carry my stuff. I needed to find my rain gear, tune up the Trek, buy new tubes and tires, and research the latest cycling-trip apps. Also, I had to accelerate my training.

The good news is I am always in spin mode somewhere, somehow, be it on the road, spin class or in my conversations, so that part would be straightforward. There's a certain definitiveness, a seriousness, when one says out loud for the first time words of such a jaunt. When you keep those plans inward, they remain a "maybe." When expressed to the world, they become a plan.

Besides my physical state, I was in decent shape, stuff wise. My bike was tuned up. I had all the cycling clothes needed, newer shoes, new Beats wireless earbuds, one extra tire and several tubes. All I had to get was a smaller handlebar-mounted cell phone case to keep out the elements and a collection of instant energy bars and other edibles for those moments when both are mandatory.

The plan came together quickly, and training was regular and challenging. There was one problem, hills. I knew there are hills, especially in central and northern Michigan, and I live in Chicago. The only hills we have are called overpasses. I also needed to get reaccustomed to riding with this added weight, approximately 20, or so, pounds. That is like having a 1-year-old baby on the back, maybe with less squiggling. It depends how well you tighten the bolts back there, I guess. I figured I could work my way up toward the first challenge as I rode through Michigan. Second, I knew I needed to reintroduce myself to the vagaries of more weight. Both were manageable. I would have it covered.

Just prior to my "Go" date, I reached out to Tom and Mary, the leadership of Danny Did Epilepsy Foundation, gauging interest of me using my ride to help their cause. Danny Did was started after the passing of Danny Stanton, a beautiful 4-year-old boy with epilepsy who lost his life from a seizure in his sleep. The outcome from this devastating event was this foundation's creation and mission to provide individuals with seizure monitors, providing families with the notifications that are so important. We quickly developed a plan.

I was ready to hit the road.

Hanging in Chicago, post–training ride

Chicago Bike Path

DAY ONE

Lobsterfest

It was "Go Time" the day before Labor Day. My starting point was Lincoln Park in Chicago.

I live only two blocks from the site of—and almost a hundred years after—the infamous St. Valentine's Day Massacre. In 1929, "Scarface" Al Capone tried to snuff out the George "Bugs" Moran "North Side" gang, igniting a gang war of gang wars. With that random thought in mind, thinking Chicago has learned little in the near century following, my plan was to head out pre-dawn during the quiet hours, take the Chicago bike path as far south as it goes, hook up with the Marquette Greenway that skirts south around Gary, Indiana, and roll into Michigan City in time for lobster. The plan pretty much worked. Saying my good-byes and promises to be safe, something that raises a tiny smile knowing I control maybe 13 percent of that safety and fate the other 87 percent, I rolled out of my Chicago Greystone, down the steps, and headed toward Fullerton Avenue and the lake. On Lake Michigan's shore, I jumped on the lakefront path heading south.

The city was just waking up. The sun was auditioning for the day, well below the horizon, just enough to light the way. The bike path is one of the best in the United States. Constructed several years ago, it was redone, thanks to politically squeezed hedge-fund money, in a divided manner separating cyclists and runners, and stretching the entire length of Chicago proper, a full 27 miles. It winds, always along the lake, through sections of Loyola University, down to Lincoln Park, Monroe Harbor and the downtown area, through the

Museum campus, further south toward Burnham Harbor, and South Shore finishing around 95th Street.

Each mile south brings you through fascinating Chicago history. In Lincoln Park, you are reminded of the Al Capone gangland wars and the strange fact that the park once was a cemetery all the way to the lake. When coffins and bodies started to wash up on shore after heavy rains, the cemetery was moved out of the park to higher ground.

Crossing the Chicago River and the downtown area, you think of the original people who settled this area: the Miami, Illinois, Ottawa and Potawatomi tribes, as long as 10,000 years ago. Like today, this area was a centralized location of a vast trading network stretching from Canada down to the Gulf of Mexico.

Further south, as you ride through the Museum campus, you are struck by the fact that most of this remarkable land was created for the 1933 Century of Progress World's Fair. It was the $200 million of revenue from that fair that sustained Chicago during the difficult years during the Depression.

Five miles further south was the site of the 1893 World's Columbian Exposition, centered around Jackson Harbor. The fact that Chicago could complete on time and attract 27 million visitors two decades after the Great Chicago Fire, which destroyed a large chunk of the downtown and northside regions of the city in 1871, was truly remarkable.

On that day, the wind was light and the temperature cooler but perfect. The sun announced its plans for the day with that burst above the horizon. Few cyclists or walkers were out. That would change in an hour or so, especially given the holiday weekend, but I would be well on my way by then.

Riding across the Calumet River on the far southeast side, 20 miles behind me already, in the shadow of the Chicago Skyway Bridge, on 95th Street, I knew at some point I wanted to hook up with the Marquette Parkway. That area was the strong blue-collar underbelly of Chicago, long known for its steel mills and refineries, most long gone now, but still carrying that toughness the area is known for.

Riding south one gets the idea of what all of Chicago was like millenniums ago, as you pass backwaters, marshes and small lakes. Ten thousand years ago, all of this was a receding massive glacier, leaving in its wake an immense body of water, much larger than today. The contraction and expansion of these waters over the next several thousand years resulted in the great beaches, dunes and back waters seen today.

Leaving Chicago proper, the path takes you across Wolf Lake, divided by I-94, and past beautiful white swans and huge flocks of geese. A lone windsurfer tried to get lift, but the winds were not yet cooperating. Maybe later. This path is worth the price of admission as it cuts across the water in a setting more reminiscent of the Everglades than far northwest Indiana. The sun was low on the horizon but in full array, a random cloud but a memory. I was the lone cyclist, lone person for that matter, as I hummed across the wooden slats of the inter-island bike path.

Across Wolf Lake, I got my first dose of what I could expect from Google Maps and Garmin. I knew where I wanted to ultimately end up, but I was a little uncertain as to how to connect from B to C to catch the Marquette Greenway. I just knew I did not want to go "that way"—the way Google wanted me to go. That way was through a series of tough neighborhoods, boarded-up houses and broken glass, lots and lots of glass all over the streets and roads. I did that route a couple of years earlier, without GPS, and getting lost, I stopped at a Gary firehouse. Pulled up in front I noticed a firefighter standing outside. He had those broad shoulders and touches of gray in the temples that told you he was either in charge or should have been. He immediately questioned my mission. With the same scrunched up face and narrowing eyes that I last saw in my own household a month earlier when describing this actual endeavor, he questioned where I was heading.

The back and forth was something like this:

"Where are you going?"

"I'm going to Michigan City."

"You're going where?"

"I'm going to Michigan City."

"How fast can you pedal?"

"I can pedal pretty fast."

"You're gonna have to!"

He then proceeded to describe the short way, and the long way, to Michigan City and advised me against the short way. I took the short way. I made it successfully, nonetheless, but that memory stuck with me, and influenced my desire to find the Greenway path, and quickly.

Since that last trip, great people doing the right thing for humankind put together all their financial and civic muscle to create this bike route from southeast Chicago, around Gary through the Indiana Dunes National Park, and ultimately into Michigan. The idea, now close to completion, is to be able to ride from north of Chicago to Bridgman, Michigan, and beyond, via a connected path of 100 miles. The Marquette Greenway itself will be at least 60 miles once completed. Ultimately, the dream is to connect Chicago all the way up to the Mackinac Bridge. I love it when civic leaders, philanthropists and bike people figure things out.

As did I. I finally found the Greenway link. As you can imagine, the path is new, or newer, and flat, and just seems to go on forever. It is not until you get up to the Indiana Dunes National Park, along the southern rim of Lake Michigan, that you notice the subtle change to rolling and shifting sand dunes, tall dune grass, lush wetlands, quiet woodlands, multi-colored native flowers and rich forests of pine and oak. Riding through the National Park, the Greenway got even more federal money to divert from a mostly monotone stretch to one where you find yourself riding through beautiful canopies of vast flora diversity. In addition, these same wise people have upgraded the rail lines and stations to make these stops bike-friendly and inviting.

The Park was christened only a few years ago, in 2019, from National Lakeshore to National Park status. Being only one of 63 national parks, it is like the medal of honor for parks, a big deal, though I sense it is still getting its sea legs with this distinction.

Indiana Dunes runs 15 miles along Indiana's northwestern coast, and with its striking plant, bird and habitat diversity, it is a must-stop, especially on bike.

Six hours after hitting the Chicago pavement, I rolled into Michigan City, which you can tell by its name, is in Indiana. I was looking for an Indiana City in Michigan, but I guess Michigan never got the joke. I figured they wanted to get even.

Michigan City combines time-gone-by blighted visuals seen throughout the Midwest with great lakeside super-homes and new commercial offshoots sprouting up in the form of small-batch breweries, cannabis shops, casinos, outlet malls and other accepted vices. Riding into town, I passed the Indiana State Prison, barbed wire and all, highlighting the days of old. With its most notorious inmate, John Dillinger, and large rows of Civil War-style gravestones, you know there is history there, but times are changing in Michigan City. With Indiana deciding to combine three crumbling old prisons into one massive new one, this relic is going away. Michigan City would love to put this tainted past behind them and emphasize the new and cool. They are getting there.

Another interesting piece from their past is Jean Baptiste Du Sable, founding father of Chicago fame, was living and arrested in Michigan City by the British military in 1779, accused of being an American sympathizer. His response of "Vous etes des idiots fous" ("You are crazy idiots") did not help his case, I guess.

It is a nice community though, always trying to redefine itself, and they have an impressive Lobsterfest tradition. At least my friends do. I figured this would be a fantastic way to kick off my ride. Julie and

Lobsterfest

5

Mary and spouses, Pat and Paul, have offered up a great tradition for several years, around Labor Day, of cooking lobster, corn and other amazing party favorites, and I was ready to go.

This was especially the case as the last six miles into Michigan City was on that dreaded, bad, crushed and not-so-crushed limestone. On limestone paths like what I was attempting to attack, tires spin and sink in the muck, especially with added weight on the back. Eventually I found black asphalt to finish my route. I understand this last blacktop leg is all that remains to finish the Greenway's completion. Good.

I arrived at a houseful of Labor Day weekend partiers. Others were still making their way back from the beach, faces aglow from the day's sun. Most were surprised by my method of transportation, curious as to my why and where, all the time welcoming me with food and drink of all types. I settled in, enjoying my defenseless lobster and my cycling water—what others call wine—and the barrage of differing conversations all voicing at once with friends and family.

I expected to hang through actual Labor Day, the next day, and was consuming accordingly. It was then I happened to glance at the weather report for the next few days. Yikes, it looked nasty. As Charlie Brown felt with the rain cloud over his head, I looked at a forecast that would repeat itself often on this trek, that of rain, often nonstop rain.

I had an opportunity to get ahead of this one. This part of Lake Michigan does give you some notice as the weather patterns move, predominantly, from west/southwest to east/northeast across the lake. This area is known for its significant snow belt, generated from moisture over the lake, and it is true for rain also. Announcing my change of plans to family and friends, I set departure early the next morning, and went back to the festivities.

Going northeast into Michigan, you are now officially in Harbor Country. Southwest Michigan is a treasure trove of great beaches, bike paths, harbor towns, decent roads, a huge array of vacation rentals and great breweries. The fields are a combination of corn, barley, apples, grapes and then pretty much everything else. From the state line to Muskegon, located in the central part of Michigan along the lake, there are at least seven harbor towns. Most, if not all, of these offer great sailing and boating destinations. The bike paths are newer, interconnected and go on for miles. Most paths go right past those microbreweries and wineries referred to earlier, which I was determined to explore further. To say there were 20, or even 25, breweries in this stretch could be a gross understatement.

The beaches are some of the finest in the United States. They encompass broad, auburn-sandy swaths, protected offshore by dune grass and newer-growth forest. Finest in the summer, that is. Not as much, starting in November. That is when the ice shelf starts to form amidst the winter snow and cold, and the crowds are no longer. Compared to the two coasts, crowds are not an issue most of the time anyway, even in the summer, but year-round these beaches are the Midwest's best kept secret.

Another, not-as-pleasant secret is every five to seven years or so, the lake levels rise, pretty much with a random regularity, and beaches rescind and shrink, and impatient homeowners panic, spending huge amounts of money trying to put a finger in the dike by building revetment walls that won't last. After the money is spent, the lake levels drop and all is back to where it was, except the ugly stone and metal walls left behind.

There are two factors most scientists attribute to the rise and fall of lake levels: the amount of frozen lake in the winter, thus affecting the rate of evaporation and precipitation, as well as the varied flows from St. Mary's River far up north, which connects Lake Superior with Lake Huron. In some years, the lake may get up to 95 percent iced over, and other years a fraction of that. Also, the amount of moisture from Canada and Lake Superior greatly influences lake levels in Lake Michigan, and ultimately the homeowners on the lake.

Despite these factors and other influencers such as El Nino and La Nina, the rise and fall of the lake levels has a regularity to it.

The area, also, has become a vacation and second-home hotspot, especially since the Pandemic, where people fled Chicago and other metropolises and realized they liked the idea of living in a small town, hanging out in their pajamas and not seeing their boss every day. This area took a hit after the great financial crash, but it has seen a true renaissance since the Pandemic, both with new homes and the renovation of existing homes.

All of this, and the forecasted hurricane, of course, was why I was anxious to get on my way. Leaving by yourself or leaving a single loved one is different than leaving a house full of people, each with their own joke, comment, story or question. You must plan for this which I did not. The clock was ticking. Finally, to no one and everyone, I announced my leaving with a promise "to see you all on the other side!" Off I rode. Twenty feet down Lakeshore Drive I felt my first drop.

DAY TWO

Margaritaville

My plan was to try to make it to South Haven, Michigan, and stay there for the night. Just by the name, you can tell it is a place you want to visit. With a population of only 4,000, this and Holland, Michigan, further north, are two of my favorites. Having sailed to both countless times, both are welcoming, Margaritaville-vibe towns, on the water with a Havana day-dreaming feel. South Haven has always been a port city, first due to logging, shipping timber to Chicago and Milwaukee, then shipping passengers and freight all over, and slowly transitioning to a resort city in the early 1900s.

South Haven was called the "The Catskills of the Midwest," although that probably did not mean much to the people from the Midwest besides the fact it sounded nice. Before the sunburned, folding-chair-carrying, igloo-pulling beachcombers arrived, this was the land of Potawatomi and Iroquois. The Potawatomi were part of the alliance with the Ojibwa and the Ottawa that controlled the western half of the Great Lakes for hundreds of years until they lost the coin flip with the U.S. government and resettled in Oklahoma, Kansas and "Indian Territory." Of course, they got even, kind of, with the advent of casinos and their granted licenses.

The day would bring me through such small towns as New Buffalo, Stevensville and across the St. Joseph River, which separates the twin, but not quite twin-looking, cities of St. Joseph and Benton Harbor, north to South Haven. Great cycling the entire way, switching between parts of the Red Arrow Highway, country roads offering the best of countless red barns, apple orchards and grape

Opposite: Michigan City lighthouse

vineyards, corn as far as the eye can see, and bike paths that melt away to the horizon. The wind, of course, did not get the memo and decided to "freshen" my face with a nice 10- to 15-mph constant smack on my nose. That would be the case for the next three or four days as the wind refused to assist, in the hopes it would somehow make me stronger.

This side of the lake is blessed by two long, scenic, old-country highways that would dominate my cycling choices, the aforementioned Red Arrow Highway and the Blue Star Highway. Red Arrow was named for the 32nd Infantry of the United States Army of World War II fame, thus the red star, and runs for 21 miles between New Buffalo, at the Michigan/Indiana state line, and St. Joseph, alternating between two lanes and four. The Blue Star Highway also pays

tribute to the U.S. armed forces and runs much further, starting at the same state line further east than Red Arrow and continuing, once connected with Red Arrow, all the way up to Mackinaw City, a total of 355 miles. I would be riding on or zigzagging parallel on a series of bike paths and smaller roads next to these, for the next several days. In most cases, I would be traveling on U.S. Bike Route 35 which travels from New Buffalo to Sault St. Marie. I was psyched.

Michigan bike paths in their glory

The day was filled with a lot of head-down cycling due to the wind, with a couple of leg breaks sprinkled in, first at an old cemetery by the name of Graceland, and then outside a somewhat random Chicago Cubs bar. There was no sighting of Elvis at Graceland, but I could not help but think that the two, Graceland and the Cubs bar, somehow fit together. The two stretches, first coming into St. Joseph's and the sands of Silver Beach, and then coming into South Haven were especially stunning. The two-laned roads into both towns take you right next to the lake with beautiful homes on the right and pristine beaches on the left, punctuated by striking lighthouses in each.

My cycling day was done as suddenly I was in downtown South Haven and staring at the harbor, brewery and the Old Harbor Inn. I knew the Old Harbor Inn was the place for me as soon as I saw it. It was situated right on a wide swath of the Black River which feeds Lake Michigan, and steps from great food and beer. Plus, as another sign I was in the right place, the hotel manager runs the local bike shop. What more could I ask?

Just 45 minutes after wheeling my chariot into the Old Harbor Inn, I was sitting at the South Haven Brewpub in the Old Harbor Village, enjoying my first beer. The place had a familiarity to it and then I realized it was the same place, a decade earlier, where my daughter pulled out her fake ID, with a nervous yet wry smile upon being carded, much to my surprise. It had been a long sail from Chicago, and we had stumbled into a $2 beer happy hour, and everything came together. I praised her resourcefulness as we sat there, tired, sunburned and definitely thirsty. Here I was, years later, reminiscing and savoring the fine beer and the cheeseburger in paradise, and thinking about the next day. Rain was in the forecast. Not just rain but a 90 percent chance of rain and thunderstorms. Zeus, the Greek god and sender of thunder, lightning, rain and wind just would not let me be. It looked like he was going to be throwing his full arsenal at me.

Grand Haven lighthouses

DAY THREE

Finger of God

The next day brought me 58 miles further down the road. That doesn't seem impressive if you are Lance Armstrong, but Armstrong had cycling "medicine" and a peloton of riders in front to block the wind. All I had was a couple of great pilsners from the Brewpub the night before as my medicine, and there was no peloton to be found. At times, I was down to 12 to 13 mph, with the wind in my face.

But I was getting ahead of myself. I awoke to the weather forecast that looked like the finger of God was pointing right at South Haven, as well as that familiar rain popcorn pitter patter that I have grown to know so well.

Wrestling with "why am I doing this stupid ride anyway?" thoughts in my head, suddenly, I smelled and was reminded that they were serving blueberry pancakes and bacon for breakfast down the hall of my hotel. Once again, Knute Rockne, that tiny motivating voice in my head, won the day, as I jumped out of bed, got dressed in every piece of rain gear I was carrying, packed up the bike and headed to breakfast. I figured if things went south and I got hit by lightning or tornado-force winds, at least I would expire on a full stomach.

During breakfast, the rain looked like there was a window of opportunity, as it slacked off slightly. Talking with my hotel manager/bike shop guy, I was feeling good that it was a perfect time to hit the road, with an added benefit that Mr. HMBS told me of a better, more scenic route, worth considering. I pushed out into the overcast, sprinkling mist. Throughout the start of the day, the wind was worse than the rain, but the rain had its moments of glory. My route took me through Saugatuck, Holland and finally, into the other Haven, Grand Haven, which if you have not guessed is both grander and north of South Haven.

As you pedal, head down at 12 to 13 mph, you notice things. One is that the Michigan economy looks like it is doing okay. Granted, my input toward this observation only involved microbreweries, farm stands, gas station stores and motels, but they all looked like they were doing pretty well, based on the cars out front and general activity.

Saugatuck is a fun little town of 800-plus people and a strong art and sailing heritage. With the rain picking up, I flashed back to two decades earlier sailing into Saugatuck via the Kalamazoo River. The 12-hour evening sail west to east across the lake from Chicago had been glorious, so glorious we never charged up our boat batteries, as we hammered Springsteen, the Dead and Neil Young all night long, only to find out our batteries were, like the band, also dead. We needed those batteries to start the engine and motor our way up the curvy, winding river into Saugatuck.

There we sat, offshore and at the river mouth, no wind, no power, with the sun coming up, wondering what our next move was. Suddenly, coming in the opposite direction and toward us was a guy in a motor-mounted rowboat. He clearly outweighed the rowboat given the height of the angle the front was sticking out of the water, but we were desperate. We flagged him down and explained our predicament, hoping for assistance. What made the visual perfect, once he agreed to help and we were moving, as he pulled us up the Kalamazoo River, his boat stuck even more out of the water at close to a 45-degree angle, was his hat that read, "Shit Happens." I so wish I had had the foresight to snap a picture of this sailing clown show as we were pulled by Mr. Shit Happens, but some things are meant to be locked up inside. Twenty minutes later, our tow completed, our friend left, heading back once again in the direction of his original destination, $20 and a case of beer, richer.

Holland, 15 miles further north, is a much larger town, nestled on beautiful Lake Macatawa, with a strong, you guessed it, Dutch

Rain, road and mud

heritage. Now, of course, the Dutch were not here first. The Ottawa Native Americans were, by several millenniums. The fact that the Ottawa were not only here first, but were also converted Catholics, was extremely problematic, as the Dutch, Calvinist Protestants themselves, emigrated from the Netherlands for religious freedom and their desire to spread their version of the Word, not someone else's, to the world. The Catholic Ottawa did not fit into this narrative. Ultimately, the Ottawa people lost, and the Dutch Calvinists won.

There were a few stops in Holland. The most memorable was the

Windmill Restaurant, that, despite its unsurprising name in a town named Holland, offered great sandwiches and good, hot coffee. The fact that the rain was pelting the Windmill's windows made the coffee that much more delicious, as I savored every sip. I do not think the Windmill dated back to Dr. van Raalte's Calvinist friends from 1847, but it had to be soon after given its overall appearance and feel, but the coffee was good! There was one sign inside that made me chuckle, as it read, "I'll have a Café Mocha, Vodka, Xanax-Latte to go, please." Exactly! Given the weather, I will take two, thank you.

The ride included a couple of memorable stretches, one along the Blue Star Highway for 20 miles, through Van Buren State Park by South Haven, and another, along the Lakeshore Connector Path, which connects Holland to Grand Haven. This is one of those paths nestled in, and often covered over by tall pines and beech, oak, and cherry trees. This is native-growth forest type of stuff reaching for the sky on either side of a pristine bike path with only a few cross-road interruptions, for 20 miles. There is a phenomenon at this time of the year, so subtle you barely notice it. The white pines are slowly and silently dropping a chunk of their needles in anticipation of colder days ahead. It is like those snowflakes at the very start of a snowfall. You notice if you pay attention, as they slowly fall across the path, only to be swept up like that feather in "Forest Gump." A cyclist's nirvana.

Given the wind and rain, sightseeing was low on my list of daily activities once traveling through Grand Haven. I did notice that Grand Haven was one of the few towns where a woman was listed as one of its founders. Madeline La Framboise, a French fur trader, and her husband, Joseph, started its first trading posts.

Grand Haven is an above-average hamlet in population and size, roughly 10,000 people, and has a couple of cool red lighthouses (yes, there are two) and an attractive lakefront. Cutting my exploration of Grand Haven's past short, I knew my priorities were to get dry, get my stuff dry and dive under the covers. Sightseeing would have to wait. The incessant wind and rain had gotten to me.

There is no substitute for rest and warmth. That was my goal as I rode up to the Courtesy Court Motel. Given my list of priorities when booking a night, Courtesy Court only had one: it was located smack dab on my route. Given the rain, that was enough for me.

I should have been alerted when I noticed they were in the process of trying to sell their website domain name, but I did not care. Plus, they had a free shuttle to the casino, wherever that was. I passed on the shuttle. The miles take a toll after a while. There are three stages that a cyclist's body experiences on a long trip like this. The first stage is "I'm fine." The second is "I'm okay." And the third is "I'm a little tender." My right hip and left Achilles were living somewhere between stage two and three but I'm fine.

One notable fact about Grand Haven is that George "Baby Face" Nelson and Homer Van Meter, notorious 1930s criminals, committed their first bank robbery at a Grand Haven bank, the People's Saving Bank. Supposedly, bullet holes from that day's events can still be found in some of the neighboring brick buildings. Nelson was just trying to get a little scratch to buy a gift for his Mrs. I get it.

Dry time in the room

DAY FOUR

Changes in Latitudes, Changes in Attitudes

My goal of getting to Ludington would put another 80 miles behind me and just under 300 since leaving Chicago. This day had everything. There were tremendous new-pavement bike paths, and some of the worst, crumbling, unnerving road shoulders this side of New York City. I left around 8:45 to the same headwind of 15-18 mph I would learn to love, taking me through Muskegon, the small hamlets of Whitehall and Pentwater, and finally into Ludington. Parts of Muskegon had the same look as the destitute parts of Gary with stretches of boarded-up houses, crumbling streets, and the general feeling of being left behind. It was evident on this cycling trip through the various towns and cities, where the city fathers and mothers decided to put their emphasis and where they did not. Some towns were more swayed by appearance focused on recreation, others more influenced by industry and commercial interests.

In Muskegon, I could not help but notice one house that I passed that had the words "House for Sale" and a phone number spray painted on the side of the actual house. I applauded the outside-the-box real estate angle, but I questioned the effectiveness. Muskegon had an industrial edge that resonated all around town as well as Muskegon Lake to its north. This was surprising as much of what I had seen, once in Michigan, had been that of repositioned harbor towns and vacation hamlets. A few miles north, or as Jimmy Buffett so succinctly wrote in "Changes in Latitudes, Changes in Attitudes" I was back in Margaritaville as my travels brought me to the vacation hamlets of Whitehall and Montague.

Whitehall and Montague to its north are beautiful vacation towns nestled on White Lake, which should be a destination, whether you are sailing, power boating, cycling or driving. The harbor is just stunning. Right after Whitehall, I hooked on to a 25-mile stretch of bike paths, including the Hart Montague Bicycle Trail, which made my day. Up to that point, the lack of live wildlife had been surprising. I say live because there had been a constant stream of dead wildlife along the roads, but not much alive. I did have the fortune to spook an owl with a decent sized snake in its talons, and a rafter of 10 to 12 wild turkeys with their heads all popping up at the same time as I passed, but few sightings of deer or anything carnivore. With the trip still young, I was still hoping as I traveled north.

As had been mentioned, the wind had never been off my face since leaving Chicago, and this day was cold as well. I had bought a cycling hoodie in Holland, and it became invaluable as it protected me from those north winds hitting my helmet and heading south, chilling me to the core. The rain, not to be left out, started up mid-ride and slowly increased from mist to moderate rain as I approached Ludington. Couple that with the last seven miles into Ludington consisting of bad, crumbling roads with heavy traffic to my left, and the final leg into town was slightly memorable. That stretch was the most unnerving of the trip so far. Constant potholes and cracks that jarred your hands, rain spray off the numerous semis and the general chill made me just want to get there.

Then that feeling, the first one of the trip, that I was losing air. Yes, an F-L-A-T, that unspeakable word, and of course, it was the back tire. I was a half-mile from Ludington, had endured 79½ miles up to that point of strong winds, then wind and rain, bad roads and streams of truck spray, and that was how the biking gods were going to reward me. What does not kill you makes you stronger.

My only choice was to walk that last half mile into Ludington, now filthy to the max, and complete the greasy tire change once I was secured at my next stop, the Logger Motel. As a rule, you never mention your bike, your bike needs or the condition of your bike to the motel office manager. It's more of a "don't ask, don't tell" kind of thing. You figure they already noticed your filthy outfit so why push the point. I did have one manager, without explanation, hand me a single bed sheet when checking in once, which I found interesting, but generally they know what I am doing and where the bike is going, so no words on this fact are exchanged.

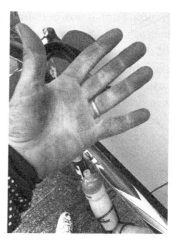

All in a day's work.

Walking my bike to the motel, which took me through downtown Ludington, and just wanting to get there and start the process of taking off the panniers, cage and back tire without touching the greasy chain—which is impossible, by the way—and then fix the flat, I could not believe my eyes. A block from my motel was the best sight all day. It was a bike shop, the Trailhead Bike Shop, to be specific. Walking closer, I saw their hours printed on the front door and saw that they closed at 6 p.m. A quick glance at my phone and it read 6:04. No-o-o! I gently knocked on the locked door, and waited, hoping some soul was still there, when David, the manager, came to the door.

It must have been my sorrowful sea captain, away-from-home-too-long appearance or that abandoned-puppy look in my eyes that made him unlock his door and ask, "Can I help you?" Another bike shop to the rescue. I am sure that was not how David wanted to end his day, but cyclist and bike shop owners have a special bond that is deeper than most religions, and he came to the rescue, less than half the time it would have taken me. Up on the rack, stuff off, tire off, he had it changed faster than you could say Ludington Loggers three times. Thanking David more than probably seemed necessary, I left with a smile on my face, and David, with a little more beer money than he had in his pocket at 6:03.

The Logger Motel was like most motels so far, except for two things. First, it was conveniently situated on Ludington's main street, surprisingly named Ludington Avenue, a block from the confluence of the Pere Marquette Lake and the Pere Marquette River, which is the channel that connects to Lake Michigan. Besides the drizzle, it was a beautiful setting. As you can tell by the fact that his name is everywhere, Father Marquette got around, as his name pops up all over northern Michigan. He reportedly died there in 1675 on his way to St. Ignace and was laid to rest where downtown Ludington now resides. I say, "reportedly," because a few other towns, including St. Ignace, claim to house the same remains. I will let them figure it out.

Second, the manager's appearance made me do a double-take as he was the spitting image of Chris Elliott, of *Schitt's Creek* and *Something About Mary*, fame. He had those things on his face seen in *Something About Mary* when Wiggy spilled the beans about his love for Mary, and he had that indescribable look that made me very nervous about walking to my room. Yet, the room was $55 for the night, a new low, so after double-locking the door, positioning the chair on the door handle, and closing the blinds, all was fine.

Before the flat, but after most of the miles were behind me, I had made the decision that I was going to have a low-mileage day the next day and start around noon, so I went in search of food and beer, finding both at Jamesport Brewing. I could not help but look a few times over my shoulder, on the way to Jamesport, for any Chris Elliott look-alikes but all turned out well.

Ludington is well known for its car ferry—the S.S. Badger—which, if in town, cannot be missed. At a length of 410 feet, a height of more than 100 feet and a beam of almost 60 feet, it stands out, to say the least. The Badger is the last steam/coal vessel of its size in the United States and the last of the 14 ferries still in operation out of Ludington. With that, it has been designated as a National Historic Landmark. It can carry up to 180 cars, buses and RVs as well as 620 passengers on a single trip.

A few years earlier, I had been up this way riding around and decided to take the ferry across to Manitowoc, Wisconsin. That was a trip. I was one of three cyclists going across that day. Leaving port, the wind was a solid 20 to 25 knots, and the waves were building to a height of 8 to 10 feet, but this monster and its 7,000-horsepower engines plowed through those waves with only a minor roll with each wave.

The trip took the expected four hours, of which half were spent walking all over the ship, including the fore deck as we rolled left-to-right, and a half-hour period playing Trivial Pursuit against other boatmates. I came in second, mind you, thanks to the help of my two 90-something tablemates who obviously spent considerable time watching *Jeopardy*, when not boating. They were a little weak on Current Events and Contemporary Music, but I was happy with our second-place free-coffee coupon. I hope the future shines kindly on the Badger to remain in operation because it is quite an experience.

T-Rex #1. Be careful out there.

DAY FIVE

Hills

I awoke the next morning, remembering that I had designated it as a "half day" and I could relax. I was relieved to know that despite certain similarities to a known actor who goes by the name Wiggy, no axe murderers showed up in the middle of the night. I could unlock both locks and remove the chair off my doorknob. All was good. Also, I was stunned by two other things I will just call "sunshine" and "a south wind." Since entering Michigan, both were foreign agents.

The sun was shining with hardly a cloud in the sky, and the flags were all pointing north in a gentle, southerly breeze, meaning, for the first time in a long time, I would have the wind at my back. With time to spare in the morning, I went looking for a good breakfast joint. I found it at Brenda's Harbor Café. They specialize in breakfast and have a relaxing view of the harbor.

As I sat there, eating my full breakfast array, and watching as the S.S. Badger shoved off, on its way to Manitowoc, Wisconsin, I noticed the North Breakwater Lighthouse in the far distance out on the lake. I knew I had more lighthouses in front of me, but the ones around Ludington are special. Some of the well-known ones nearby are Big Sable Point, North Pierhead and Little Sable Point, but this ride was filled with great lighthouses all the way around.

This was a perfect start to the day. Repacked and ready to go, tires fixed and full, sun out, and wind kissing me from behind, I decided to start at the Ludington Beach, the North Breakwater Lighthouse in the background. The cycling gods were finally smiling. This was after Labor Day, and a weekday. The beaches were mostly empty, only a few stragglers hanging out on a beautiful September day, and the parking lot was maybe 10 percent full.

The rest of the world was back at work. Heading out, Lakeshore Drive beckoned me north. I knew, especially with this favorable wind, that this day could be a shorter and faster day. My target was Frankfort, approximately 70 miles north. I got a later start than I had planned, as breakfast and a quick stop back at Trailhead Bike put me behind schedule. I hit the road at 1 p.m., the full sun heating me up instantly.

The only unknown worrying me would be the hills. For the first time since starting, hills would be a factor. Checking out my route, there were at least three steep climbs of several hundred feet each, and a total ascent of more than 1,600 feet. Again, world-class triathletes would laugh at the idea of even mentioning hills, but I'm a kid from Chicago with no hills within 200 miles, and I was carrying an additional 20 pounds, not including the bike and me.

I have done hills in the past. Cycling through the Green Mountains of Vermont and the White Mountains of New Hampshire come to mind, as do cycling trips from Seattle to Portland, and the bluffs of Minnesota that go in and out, and up and down around the Mississippi River. But none happened after that Medicare card arrived in my mailbox. I knew there were two to three more days of hills ahead. This was going to be a good first test.

From Lakeshore Drive in Ludington, my Google Maps for cyclists and my Garmin announced a stream of zigs and zags, first north, then east, then north again, mostly on nice two-lane state highways. One memorable stretch included Hwy 110 and Crescent Beach Road, which was as nice as it sounds. The hills were still in the distance, so I rode on, constantly in react mode as new instructions came across my earbuds.

Then Garmin stopped working and Google took on a mean streak. It kept insisting that I take a certain 8-mile road north that at first sight looked terrible. It was that dreaded dirt road, obviously under construction, and looking hilly. Hills and loose gravel roads are not a good combination. I had no alternative but to retrace my route and find a paved—and longer, mind you—course in which to ride.

Throughout the trip, I would experience this a number of times, usually at the worst possible moments, where Google Maps and Garmin would recommend a road that was gravel, pot-holed and terrible for my tires, not to mention me.

In my ears, my kind friends would keep insisting their way was the right way. My eyes told me differently. Ultimately, I had to just turn off the noise and trust my instincts.

The first real hill was a shocker. It was a mile grind, where I ultimately was forced into my lowest granny gear, apologies to all grandmas, as

Solo silhouette north of Ludington

I rode in and out of the saddle, standing on my pedals at the steepest points. The peak grade, as announced by my now-working Garmin, was 11 percent and the road just kept going higher and higher, as I rounded one corner left, the next corner right, and then left again, back and forth until finally the summit was in sight.

My Garmin seemed to especially enjoy telling me the distance to the summit, as well as the ascent grade percentages, as I grinded harder. I have determined there are evil people working at Garmin who do not venture outdoors much and want to punish those who do.

The second major hill was right after the first, barely enough time to catch my breath from the last climb. That one was a 7-percent grade, and almost as long. I pushed through. The important thing is that you cannot stop during these climbs, or you are doomed. You must keep moving forward. If you stop at these grades, you will never be able to restart on the bike and will end up walking. My pride would never let me accept walking. Never.

Also, this was the first warm day of the ride. The temperature reached the low 80s, and with those hills, I was spraying sweat. I am typically not a huge water drinker on these rides, but I had fortunately refilled my water bottles and grabbed an extra two at an Exxon station prior to the hills. I finished off number four after summiting the third hill, another 7-percenter, and would go through six by the end of the day.

With the late start, re-routings and the hills, I rode into Frankfort later than I had wanted, fearful that the Bay Lodge Motel office would be closed. Thankfully, all was good, as Tammy smiled and handed me my room key. I went through my litany of questions regarding peculiarities related to the room, good places to eat and all things Frankfort-related. Frankfort is a small harbor town of 1,200 that also stakes the claim that Father Marquette died there.

There are always peculiarities related to the room, I have discovered. Some, the motel staff tell you about, while others, well, you find out on your own. I would discover this hotel's peculiarities later that evening. After more chatting, this time with other Bay Lodge Motel patrons sitting out in front of their rooms enjoying a plate of cheese and crackers and a glass of Chablis, I knew time was getting away from me. I quickly got cleaned up and headed a few blocks away to where all the restaurants were located. My Bay Lodge lady had given me several raving reviews of the restaurants in town, so I walked quickly in anticipation. The first one turned out to be closed. This never came up from Tammy back at the motel. The second one was also closed. I guessed no one needs to eat in Frankfort on Tuesdays.

The third was open, but the teenager behind the greeting stand told me the kitchen was closed for the night, being after 8 p.m., and was not accepting any other customers. I pleaded my case, but it became quickly evident I had zero chance of eating there that night. I was running out of options, and I was starving, given the calories burned that day.

An unexpected feature with the Garmin was it volunteered the number of calories burned during the day, with the number being just under 5,000 that day. Who knows how it figured this out, but right at that moment I was in full belief. I needed food. Walking a couple more more blocks in despair, it became obvious that my only option left was a run-down, take-out-only pizza place, so I walked across the street and got in line. And I waited. And waited. I did not know that the three people in front of me were the Frankfort High School Panthers football coach and a couple of his players. They had just ordered 20, yes 20, pizzas for the entire team, so I stood there, and stood there. Finally, as I watched this small staff scurrying around like they had just gotten the announcement that the Titanic was sinking and to quickly find a lifeboat, one teenage girl interrupted her scurrying and asked, "Can I help you?" Seeing this as my opportunity, I quickly ordered an Italian sub sandwich with the works, and then patiently waited for the 20 pizzas to come to completion, and on their way to one hungry football team.

Standing there with little else to do but observe, you got the impression this may have been their largest pizza order ever, or at least since the last time the football team showed up. Timing is everything. Finally, sub in hand, I found a park bench, staring out at the harbor, sun safely down below the horizon by this time, and ate my dinner, in lonesome retreat. With no possibility for that single libation, and the town virtually shut down, I walked back to the Bay Lodge.

The peculiarity I mentioned earlier had to do with the room air conditioning. The room had been warming all day, and had stayed warm and humid into the night. Getting back to my room, the temperature had to be 85. That was okay, I thought, because I had a window air conditioner. Unfortunately, it looked like it had been built right after the war—the Second World War. Undeterred, I pressed the "ON" button and stepped back. The sound was not too dissimilar to a small passenger jetliner taking off in your backyard.

"This can't be," I said out loud, to no one in particular.

"How can I sleep?" I turned it off.

Laying down, the sauna started to crank. I turned it on. That sound again. I turned it off. This pattern continued late into the night until, somehow, I fell asleep with the pillow over my head.

Riding through nirvana

DAY SIX

Sleeping Bear Dunes

The morning could not come soon enough. I was bushed from those hills the day before and the jet engine sounds the previous night, and I did not want to stay in that room any more than necessary, so I packed up and rolled the Trek Terror out the door, right at 7 a.m. in anticipation of good food and coffee. Tammy had mentioned Bella's Café, and Birch and Maple, as two decent breakfast stops, with the passing remark that "I am not sure what time they open."

Given my undersized dinner from the night before, I needed substance. I figured one of the two would work. Going to Bella's first, it was closed, and it looked like it had been closed for many more than just one day. I started getting that sinking feeling again. I decided to try Birch and Maple. Walking up to the front door, it clearly stated that it did not open until 9 a.m. What breakfast place opens at 9 a.m.? That was two hours away. Damn. It looked like I am going back to the gas station. Which is exactly what I did.

"One re-heated Morning Terror cup of coffee and that donut-looking thing in the plastic to go, please."

I was not deterred.

"Today will be a great day," I thought, putting my thoughts of sustenance behind me, "Sleeping Bear Dunes and Traverse City here I come."

I failed to mention one other thing as I inhaled my coffee and donut-thing at the gas station. It was misting. It was the type of mist where 50 percent of the car drivers would not even flip on their wipers. But for a cyclist, it's just annoying, and a subtle reminder that maybe I had actually landed in an alternate universe, a multiverse, and was really biking through the Amazon, not northern Michigan. Doing a trip like this, one is in an alternate universe, just by its nature, but this rain-thing was getting old.

Despite the annoyance, I hit the road and pedaled on, first heading east out of town, on a truly magnificent 10-mile bike path, the Betsie Valley Trailway, that weaved around tall, lush green forests and placid ponds and streams. The path alternated between blacktop and wooden bikeways, back and forth, crossing multiple small streams, waterfalls, and marsh. I never saw another human the whole 10 miles, which is fine, as the tranquility was stunning, and it set my head right for the fun I was anticipating up north.

Speaking of fun, with 10 miles done and the morning still young, I took a straight turn due north heading to the town of Empire, and then Sleeping Bear Dunes, a national lakeshore with stunning sand dunes close to 500 feet high. I passed several amazing-looking golf courses, one of which, Arcadia Bluffs, is in the Top 100 golf resorts nationally. I will play that one someday. I passed so many great courses it was hard to count, most with impeccable green fairways, and fabulous forested, rolling hill settings. As tempting as all of that looked, I was still on my mission, and I knew what laid ahead, the rain expected, and the hills coming up.

Because they have not been mentioned in the last few pages does not mean the hills went away. Just the opposite. As tough as the previous day was, this day's hills were even harder. The heat was gone, but the rain made them even more challenging. The stated vertical for the day, thanks to "Karen," from Garmin was 2,850 feet, over a half mile of climb. Just like the previous day, I was forced out of my seat, standing on the pedals for power, pumping in low gear, the back-end swaying with each stroke like there was a sleeping baby attached just ready to wake up. You just have to try to keep going. Finally, in front of me was the sign for the town of Empire, the official gateway to Sleeping Bear Dunes, as highlighted by their town sign announcing such fact. Looking around, there was no sign of Darth Vader, Luke or Chewy.

Entering Sleeping Bear Dunes

Any town, or in this case, village, of 362, that calls itself "Empire" you figure there must be a story. The reason for this small hamlet to carry such a majestic name goes back to 1865 when a schooner named Empire became icebound, permanently stuck for the winter, and the locals decided that was a cool name for the village. For most places up this way, lumber was the trade, typically carried on schooners, until coal and steam became the new thing.

I was determined to seek out Sleeping Bear because I really wanted to see it from the vantage point of a bicycle. Years earlier I had sailed in these waters with a friend, Hawk, and my three kids and his two, and it was such an amazing sailing trip that I wanted to see it up close from the other side. We had sailed across from Door County on the Wisconsin side and dropped anchor in the deep waters right off South Manitou Island. It was a majestic night as we lay in 80 feet of water only 50 yards from shore, grilling and chilling, as a lightning show blew by to our west. To our east rose the stunning dune of Sleeping Bear.

The Manitous are two islands just to the northeast off Sleeping Bear Dunes. The park's name is based on the Ojibwa legend about the sleeping bear. According to the legend, an enormous forest fire along the shore of Lake Michigan drove a mother bear and her two cubs into the lake for safety. The exhausted cubs ended up drowning in the lake, but the mother bear stayed and waited, hoping her cubs would finally appear. Impressed by the mother bear's faith and determination, the Great Spirit created two islands to commemorate the cubs, and the winds buried the sleeping bear under the sands of the dunes where she waits to this day.

The park consists of a 35-mile stretch along Lake Michigan that includes those vast dune formations, deep native growth forest, great hiking and biking paths, beaches, and stunning glacial remnants. "Good Morning America" named it the most beautiful spot in America, and Congress designated a part of the park as the Sleeping Bear Dunes Wilderness. I could not know all of this and not check it out.

Michigan, at only the 15th most forested state in the country, is still 55 percent covered in forests with more than 20 million acres. Where I was riding, between northern Michigan and the Upper Peninsula, it seemed I had ridden through 90 percent of the 55 percent. Everywhere I went, apart from the various harbor towns, it seemed like I was in the middle of a national, state, county or private forest, populated with sugar maple, American beech, white and red oak, and pine trees.

At the same time, you cannot help but notice the large swaths of dead or dying groves, especially in the northern lowland areas impacted by the various invasive pests, such as pine and beech bark beetles, spruce budworm, oak wilt, and emerald ash borers, all taking their toll. Many experts estimate that half of all oaks in the state are vulnerable to disease presently and could add to the likes of elm and chestnut on the list of trees disappearing from Michigan.

Most scientists attributed this demise to acid rain or drought, which weakened the trees and then the invasive bugs that took advantage. Pure water has a pH of 7.0. Normal rain has a pH of 5.5. The U.S. Geological Survey reported the acidity of precipitation in Michigan as 4.9 to 4.4, or 100 times more acidic than normal rain. This acid impacts the ability of trees to grow and fight disease. A redeeming quality for these Great Lakes' states is the filtering effect these large bodies of water produce that counteracts some of this negative impact. Given all of this, plus the history of over-logging that took out centuries of old pine and hardwood back in the early 1900s, the Forest Service has its work cut out.

The road from Empire to the Dunes Overlook is about 6 miles, half of which, or more, is on the Sleeping Bear Heritage Trail and then the Pierce Stocking Scenic Drive. The roads and paths are all just stunning, carving through majestic, dark forests of beech-maple, and pine, and for the most part traveling downhill. You knew you were heading downhill for two reasons. The first is that I was not working very hard. Seems simple, but in the majesty of the woods sometimes that part does not register with you.

The second reason is more evident. There are numerous signs, each reporting a steep hill ahead. But the vast majority are all going downhill, ultimately to the lakeshore. When you get downhill after downhill your stomach starts tightening up because you know you must attack each one of those hills as you climb out on the way east to Traverse City. The path is worth the effort, but one needs to be prepared for how challenging it was going to be. I finally saw the signs for the overlook, where I dismounted and walked that last leg, in anticipation.

The rain never really stopped, again becoming more of a mist, which makes you mindful of what can happen when a slick bike path and weighted down bike meet together, but all was good as I got to the lookout. With the low-hanging clouds and storm approaching from the west, my view was limited, but I could see the dunes and lakeshore, Empire Bluffs, 4 miles to the south, along with Point Betsie 15 miles further south.

The lake narrows here and is only 54 miles across to Wisconsin, but this is tough to make out with the rain and clouds. You do not lose the fact that you are staring at the fourth largest freshwater lake in the world. A product of the Ice Age, this was formed by a great lobe of ice advancing down the continent. Signs nearby talk about the mix of sand and glacier rock, as well as the fact the dunes are losing about a foot per year, as they wear away. This is very much an active dune environment.

What was also active was the thunderstorm developing offshore and heading my way. Sightseeing was over. Time to tackle those hills. Starting back up, heading south and east, the hills were upon me. Immediately I saw signs for "Steep Hill" and then "7 Percent Grade," "10 Percent Grade" and "8 Percent Grade." Did the number of signs for "Steep Hill" just double? Is there a sign guy following me and adding signs? I did not remember all of these on the way down to the outlook.

Then the storm was upon me. The rain intensified to the point that the rain drops became blinding, stinging lasers. All I could do was keep my head positioned down and hammer away, attacking the hills as they came. The bike tires were slipping but manageable. For a guy who rode where the only hills were overpasses, I was starting to figure them out.

I had a flashback of a ride years earlier from Seattle to Portland, Oregon, where in the middle of the ride there was a deluge of blinding rain like this. I remember going downhill on a long, steep curve in a line of 8 to 10 cyclists, well over 35 miles per hour, just praying the guys in front of me and behind me kept their lines and balance.

The rain I was experiencing on this day was torrential. Another funny thing about rain and relying on instruments, like Garmin and Google Maps in my case, was when I stopped, finally out of the national forest and those hills, the rain was hitting my screens so hard while I was researching my next stop and typing, that the result was coming out as some type of Russian code, looking more Cyrillic than English. As much as I tried to cover with one hand, the results made no sense. I was back in the god-forbid pre-internet 1990s.

Finally, parked under a huge pine, I was able to lock in my

directions to Traverse City. The route had about 30 miles left, which normally was nothing, but I was bushed from the hills and rain. Looking at Google Maps, I saw a total vertical climb of 1,650 feet still to go, with two more bigger climbs and one huge one outside of Traverse. That last one looked long and had more than 500 feet of ascent. That seemed rather unnecessary, and a little mean. Oh, well. Onward.

The rain normalized, if that is possible or even a thing, over the big chunk of the stretch from Sleeping Bear eastward, but it started to really intensify once I was on that last big hill, and it continued unabated all the way into Traverse City. I had no motel reservations in the city. I had attempted to research places to stay, but that was when the rain was conversing with the Russians, so it became impossible. I just decided to wing it. The rain was stupid at this point, as I rode into town along Route 72 amidst the shores of Traverse Bay, with huge rivulets flowing down the streets, sometimes submerging my cycling shoes. It was then that the Country Inn appeared in front of me, and I knew this was home for the night, if they would have me.

My bike parked outside, I walked to the front desk. The first thing I saw on their lobby TV, situated directly behind the front desk, in big letters, was *"Flash Flood Warning."* "Yeah...thanks for the update."

I must have been a sight. There is no way to hide that I just rode through a river. The lady behind the counter just laughed, and said, "Did you ride in this storm?"

Trying to think of something witty, I said, "Ye-e-e-p."

"Where are you coming from?" She then asked, scrunching her face.

"Frankfort, by way of Sleeping Bear. I know it sounds stupid. Sounded better when I got up this morning," was all I could muster.

"Oh my God," was her mustered response. Shaking her head back and forth, she quickly concluded our conversation with the words, "Room 114."

Traverse City was originally called "Gichiwiikwedoongsing" by the Ojibwa, meaning the head of the great bay, but quickly shortened because none of the Native Americans could pronounce

Riding in flash flood warnings

the original name, I am just guessing. Of course, names tended to change once the Europeans showed up. French voyageurs changed it to Grand Traverse after the grand traverse, or long crossing, across the mouth of the bay, and it stuck. In 1852, some lady at the U.S. Post Office thought that Grand Traverse City was too long and eliminated the Grand part, thus today's name.

Traverse is only a city of 15,000, which is surprising given how well it is known. In 2015 and 2016, Traverse City was named the best small town in America by Livability.com, and I get it, riding into town. Between the rain drops, the stunning old grand houses one after the next by the shore are beautiful. This city, and this area, is also known for cherries. Cherries everything: pie, cobbler, muffins, bread, jam, wine, you-name-it. I committed myself, once I checked the weather forecast, to come back and explore TC in greater depth. The rest of the evening was uneventful, given the day I had experienced, but the hotel had a hot tub and it was close to a brasserie, which is kind of like a restaurant with lots of brass, I guess, so I was in heaven. The hot tub was amazing as it chased the chill away, but I think I barged in on a newlywed couple who were hoping for some "alone time." I cut my tubbing time short. The brasserie had a decent hamburger and a great assortment of beer. By now, walking in the rain, with the borrowed hotel umbrella, and my trusty flip flops had become second nature. Sleep could not come soon enough. The beautiful harbor towns of Charlevoix and Petoskey awaited the following day.

DAY SEVEN

Charlevoix and Petoskey

The day began like the rest, checking the weather first, but with the rarity of free breakfast as well (thank you Country Inn). Seeing that there was only a 10 percent chance of rain, and the full breakfast awaiting, loaded with sugar and carbs, spread out in front of me, I took my time and enjoyed it. Next, I checked my route options. I knew there were hills. The hills would not really end until I was safely across the Mackinac Bridge, and into the UP.

Google kindly offered 2,018 vertical feet of climb for the day and 80 miles, with the added wink of "Steep Hills" just for emphasis. Then it added, "Use caution. Bicycling directions may not always reflect real-world conditions," as if this was my first rodeo. We know. That probably took Google and a team of lawyers six months to come to the exact wording for that disclaimer. Nonetheless, the horse was fed, saddled up and ready to ride.

I have always been a little unsure what those percentages of precipitation really mean. I clearly can figure out what 100 percent means. I know 0 percent as well. It's those 10 percent or 60 percent that had me puzzled. Does that mean I will get wet 10 percent or 60 percent of the day, or only that that amount of some defined geographic space will actually get nailed?

Again, maybe those are just odds given previous days with similar setups. I do not know. All I know is that the aforementioned 10 percent became 100 percent pretty much two miles down the road after leaving the comfort of the Country Inn. Here we go again; rinse and repeat.

Opposite: Charlevoix lighthouse

At that point on my trip, I was actually happy to see my friend, Mr. Rain, for it had been much too long—12 hours at least—since we had seen each other, and I missed him dearly. I felt good knowing I was taking the bullet for the rest of the 90 percent who obviously were staying dry. This time it was more of a mist than actual rain, but I was wet, nonetheless. It was like that last stage in a car wash, the gentle spray to get that last remnant of soap off your car, or a Galway rain without the sheep.

The route brightened my mood. First heading east along the two prongs of land jutting out into Traverse Bay and along Traverse City's beautiful shoreline, my route eventually took a sharp turn left, and north. The route continued north along the east shore of Torch Lake, a finger lake to the east of Traverse Bay, past the town of Eastport and finally into Charlevoix, situated right between Grand Traverse Bay and Little Traverse Bay. The route could be summed up by two songs, Dylan's "A Hard Rain's A-Gonna Fall" and John Mayer's "Gravity." Maybe throw in a third song, "Beautiful World" by Kenny Chesney, for good measure. That gives you an idea of the day.

It was during this period of tranquility, when I was riding along past endless groves and along pristine county roads, looking around at anything and everything around me except what laid directly ahead, I was startled back to reality by a huge hump in the road that almost took me and my chariot down.

Gaining my balance, I looked back to see I had just ridden over a very large and very dead porcupine, quills and all. The thought that after days of hills, wind and rain, my demise could have been the result of a lone displaced porcupine could only bring a smile.

On the one hand, the day included beautiful corridors of rolling tall pine and oak for miles, the shore of Torch Lake to my left, thick forests to my right. The trees this far north were just starting to wink that Fall was soon approaching. These roads would ultimately transition to great bike paths along the rocky northern shores of Lake Michigan and its many bays, and their crystal-clear waters. During these stretches, I would come across small colorful villages, filled with cool shops and antique stores, begging me to stop and explore.

I wish I had a large-sized Snickers bar for every antique store I passed by on this trip. There have been a lot, possibly hundreds. They ranged from super-inviting with cool displays and old stuff worth checking out to after-thought structures with crap everywhere and no second thought as to why or where. Other stretches would include very remote, rolling-hill farms and bright red barns. Just me and the cows. They must not see a lot of cyclists because they all looked when I passed by, with that unimpressed stare, the whole time chewing away.

On the other hand, the hills between Eastport and Charlevoix were as advertised. Once again Garmin kept wanting to put me on gravel roads. Note my previous comments about hills and gravel. I am not a fan. It was a planned 80-mile day to Petoskey but with the Garmin interruptions, miles were added. Garmin and Google kept putting me on gravel roads and away from state highways or county roads I was comfortable riding.

Bridge Street bridge in Charlevoix

At one point outside of Charlevoix, I finally relented. I had no other alternative besides serious backtracking. The road, a mix between dirt and gravel, rolled on for two miles, until another paved state highway emerged to save me, back on solid paved ground for the next six miles into town.

I do think that both Garmin and Google need to produce more playthings, in their offices, like magicians or rare animal shows, so their young talent do not become bored and take it out on poor cyclists. The road names sometimes became amusing. There was one point where I was on Bunker Hill Road which took me to Hills Road and then back to Maple Hill Road. I would just save money and put up one sign stating, "Bunch of Hills Ahead Road" and leave it at that.

The ride into Charlevoix was amazing. Beautiful waters to the north and west, the town of only 2,500 is lined with tremendous painted-lady houses from days past, Victorian in style, nestled up on the hills rising from the shore. The town and its name are obviously of French origin, predominated by voyagers, loggers, and fishermen mostly, but, again, the Ojibwa and Ottawa might desire to add their piece to this story.

An interesting side note is that the residents of Charlevoix engaged in a short-lived skirmish with one James Jesse Strang, leader and namesake of the Strangite Mormons, and then self-proclaimed 'King' of Beaver Island. He was a character, to say the least, who named the first settlement on Beaver Island after himself and lobbied, successfully, to have ownership of Beaver Island granted to him and his followers. He ruled absolutely, banning polygamy among his followers but taking on five wives for himself.

Relations between Charlevoix residents and the Strangites were often tense, resulting in a gunfight between the two groups in 1853, as the townspeople refused to hand over a man called for jury duty on the island. It was known locally as the Battle of Pine River. Strang ended up getting his comeuppance as he was assassinated, mysteriously, in 1856. An ironic note was that years later, Strang's son, Charles, started one of the first real newspapers in Charlevoix, the *Charlevoix Journal*, in 1883.

Charlevoix has a long history as a summer resort destination, starting in the late 1880s and flourishing well into the 1920s with money from Chicago and further east. Later, Detroit auto money would also use this area as a prime summer destination, and second home residence. People would travel by lake passenger liners and rail service from Chicago, Cleveland, Buffalo and other Midwest locales and, eventually by automobiles. Ernest Hemingway spent many boyhood summers in this area, writing about this area around Lake Charlevoix.

During Prohibition, Charlevoix became a popular hangout for gang members from Chicago. The Colonial Club, a restaurant and gambling joint on the city's north side, became known as a popular place for the Midwest's most notorious, as well as, most powerful and influential. The club's owner, John Koch, had Michigan license plate number "2," second only to the Michigan governor, as a sign of his influence. Converted lumber barges served as speakeasies, or "blind pigs" as they were called, sailing nightly between Boyne City and Charlevoix until the Feds decided enough was enough and shut things down. I knew I liked this town as soon as I rolled in.

The town is dominated by a big red lighthouse and a single draw-bridge that rose over the connecting waterway, Pine River, which connects Lake Michigan and Round Lake, as large passenger vessels sail in and out. I chose this cool setting to grab lunch at the Bridge Street Tap Room. Bridge Street is typical of what I would see several times riding through Petoskey, Mackinaw City and other harbor towns, most filled with great bars and breweries, ice cream shops and amazing cafes.

Seated in the Tap Room, positioned at the end of a fabulous bar from days immediately after, or possibly during, Prohibition, with a view of my parked chariot outside, I settled into the warmth and dryness of indoor eating. During lunch, the typical questions of route and the "whys" came up. The back and forth became lively, usually at my expense, which I enjoyed immensely. Finishing things up, I asked a couple of people if they knew where the 17-mile bike path to Petoskey started. It always amazed me how so many people had zero clue about anything remotely involving a bicycle. I would

Bike path along Lake Michigan outside Petoskey

repeatedly get that twisted-up face, eyebrows up, I-don't-have-a-clue look as if I was asking the actual amount of the United States deficit.

With a quick look, Google was my friend this time, and the answer became evident and surprising. The path was across the street, 100 feet away, starting on the banks of Round Lake. This took me to the Little Traverse Wheelway, which would continue until a mile outside of Petoskey. Once again, if you need an answer to a local question, never ask a local. The people around the bar were otherwise nice enough, curious about my ride and if my butt hurt, and we had a fun conversation. I finally bid them adieu, walked my bike across Bridge Street and started on my journey east.

I cannot overstate how amazing this last leg was, as I weaved back and forth, always along the shoreline, on smooth blacktop. The sun had peeked out for the first time in days, so I had a shimmering sparkle off the lake to my left, that crystal water reaching down 10 to 15 feet to multicolored stones of every size and shape, slight warmth on my face. I could do this ride every day for a year and never get tired of it, apart from that brief period between November and April called Michigan winter, of course. I stopped a couple of times, just to take in the view. It was that nice.

The name Petoskey is from the Ottawa Native Americans, and is said to mean, "where the light shines through the clouds." I took this as a positive sign. I was willing to use any tool to my advantage, even if I had to hire a team of fortune tellers or spiritual healers, if that is what it would take, to bring a little sunshine back into my ride.

The Bay Inn was my day's destination, with no reservation in hand, as I walked in, once again wearing that "I lost my dog" look on my face.

"Let me look. Of course! We have a room," was the response, one I would hear repeatedly on the trip.

I was set. Located up on a hill, overlooking the waters of Little Traverse Bay, I was on the main road out of town, close to fast-food heaven, not ideal but this was day seven, and the room had a shower, free coffee and a hair dryer. Perfect. The next day was going to be a short day as I was only 40 miles or so shy of Mackinaw City. The day's challenge would be figuring out the vagaries of getting across the Mackinac Bridge, and into St. Ignace, but first I had to find a bike shop in town, which, it appeared, there were at least three. I slept soundly with bike tubes, tire levers and bike pumps in my head.

Me and the Mighty Mac

DAY EIGHT

The Mighty Mac

The start of the eighth day since I left Chicago was uneventful as I knew I had a light day, and I would be in search of a bike shop prior to exiting Petoskey. I took my time getting out the door, ate a full breakfast next door and then went on my search. The first bike shop was closed, a second did not have what I needed as they were setting up for ski season, and the third, I had to wait for them to open. The life of a bike shop owner. Why can't they be more on my schedule?

To explain my urgency for finding a bike shop, a couple of days prior, in the pounding rain, I had a couple of casualties. My small tool bag, which I opened and closed countless times in the rain lost some valuable tools like tire levers and loose Allen wrenches with me not noticing, and I wanted to replace them prior to the UP. Also, in the flash flood warning coming into Traverse, my Beats earbuds stopped working, and I hoped to find a new pair of wireless ear buds, if possible.

My day started with blue skies, amazing sights, and those dreaded north winds. That was okay, I said to myself, because it looked like I had bike paths almost the entire way to Mackinaw. After all, it was named "Green Arrow Route – Mackinac Trail," which turned into the "Petoskey to Mackinaw Trail," which sounded amazing. Just to make sure, as I was paying for my stuff at bike shop No. 3, and talking with the owner and his store sidekick about my ride so far,

I asked about the bike path ahead. They said it was crushed limestone but "okay," meaning rideable. "In fact, I rode it last week," one
of the two said.

"On skinny tires?" I asked.

"Sure, on 28s," he responded. Those were the same tire width as
mine. So far so good.

Walking outside, I ran into a third guy, who had overheard our
conversation, and was unmistakenly wearing an ankle cast from his
toes up to mid-shin, which piqued my interest.

"That path was the reason I went to the ER last week, I almost
died," he remarked, glancing down at his encased ankle. "I hit one
of those potholes." Then he added, "You do what you want." Great.
Thanks for the tip. Immediately those tiny heartburn workers started
hammering the pit of my stomach once again.

Despite the dire warning from my friend, I decided to give the
route a look. Getting to the path and not having a clear alternative, I
gave it a shot, images of ambulance rides in my head. I knew immediately I did not want to do that for 22 miles. It was wet limestone
from the days of rain before, and bumpy with difficult to see potholes here and there. It was challenging with the wind and, combined with the crummy surface, was tough to even maintain 11 to 12
mph. I needed an alternative route.

The only road going in my desired direction was Route 31, a busy
four-lane state highway under construction. Google Maps had not
gotten the memo about the construction. Also, it was down to two
lanes with construction vehicles all over and no shoulder. My pals
at the bike shop failed to mention a bit of this.

Starting my ride that morning, I had visions of a beautiful smooth
bike path all the way north, but I was faced with inventing a new way
on side roads as Google and Garmin continued to bark uninformed
directions incessantly. I ended up paralleling the construction zone
on various side streets and roads, back and forth, for several miles,
until finally the construction was behind me and I could jump on the
shoulder of Hwy 31.

Hwy 31 is usually busy, as it is the only straight-shot highway between the two points heading north to Mackinaw City, but it was especially busy while I was on it, with a bunch of pissed-off drivers who had just sat through major traffic delay and were anxious to make up for lost time. In addition, the road was out in the open with farm fields and occasional big box logistic centers as the only wind impediments. The north wind was a steady 15 mph, with gusts of 20 to 25 straight in my face. I knew the last 20-plus-mile stretch would be dreadful. It was.

All you could do was put your head down and push, plunging pedal after pedal, counting mile after mile. It may have been there where I started my tradition of celebrating every 10-mile increment with the loud exclamation of "BOOM!" in celebration of putting road behind me. Seems silly, but it gave me something to look forward to, and it worked.

With the small of my back barking, my left lower Achilles tendon once again flaring and my hands numb, I finally hit the outskirts of Mackinaw City. The first thing you see entering town is the Michigan Welcome Center, which kind of strikes you given its location. Typically, you find Welcome Centers as you enter a state, not somewhere way up north and miles away from any state border. Who exactly are they welcoming, and why here? Leaving those questions for a later date, I decided to lean my bike against the large glass windows and check it out. The Welcome Center turned out to be awesome with rows of pamphlets and maps on everything Michigan, and the staff was extremely helpful. Those people apparently love their jobs and were great ambassadors to all things Michigan, especially around Mackinaw City and Mackinac Island.

Exiting the welcome center, new maps in hand, I was even more excited to see the Upper Peninsula, and only wish this welcome center had been located 350 miles south when so much of this information would have been relevant. I know this is old school, but there is something comforting about having a physical map in your hand versus the map on your phone or Garmin. The next time it rains in Russian I can grab the paper maps and figure things out.

Mackinaw City and Mackinac Island have a deep history. At

one time or another, this area was controlled by a wide variety of nations and nationalities. The Algonquin peoples of Ojibwa, Ottawa and Potawatomi, who called it Michilimackinac, were the dominant Native Americans; then the New French took over by way of Jean Nicolet and Father Marquette and their mission; then the British next during the Seven Years' War, and then the French again and back to the British, again, after the American Revolutionary War. Then Pontiac and his rebels, a loose confederation of Native Americans, again, including Chippewa and Fox, retook the forts from the British, before ultimately being settled by American traders on their never-ending move west.

In a strange twist, Mackinac Island was designated the second official national park in the United States, right after Yellowstone, in 1875, by Ulysses S. Grant. It held that title until 1895, when the park was turned over to the state of Michigan and downgraded to a state park. Why would that happen? It appears that the park was falling in disrepair, and the federal government gave them the option to be taken over and funded by the state of Michigan or the feds would come in and take the land for good, ultimately resulting in one great trivia answer as to the name of the second-ever-named national park in the United States.

Once in town, one cannot miss the Mackinac Bridge, a five-mile long, 552-foot-high monolith. It is the longest suspension bridge between two anchorages in the Western Hemisphere, connecting Mackinaw City and St. Ignace, carrying 11,000 cars and trucks daily. The vision of a bridge connecting these outreaches had been in the works as long ago as 1884, when industrialist Cornelius Vanderbilt, inspired by the newly built Brooklyn Bridge, had wanted a means to ferry his guests to his newly built hotel.

Discussions went on for decades after, but they never could satisfy the solution for the massive winter ice that would stress the support technologies of that day. Construction finally started seven decades later in 1954 and finished on time in 1957. I find this three-year time frame amazing. Chicago, like other current day metropolises, just went through a major interstate interchange project, not even close to this bridge's complexity, and it was seven years over-due and at least twice the initial budget. The deck of the bridge's center swings as far as 35 feet east-to-west during high winds which might account for why it took so long to figure out the needed con-struction technology. It also is the reason one cannot ride their bike across the bridge and must be transported. My mission was to be one of these cyclists being transported but before I did, I wanted to explore Mackinaw City.

Mackinaw has a couple of cool things to check out, including the world's largest hot dog, located at Wienerlicious. This is a small diner serving hot dogs, brats, sandwiches and a lot more, and just happens to have a ridiculously immense hot dog structure on its roof dwarfing the actual diner. Also, one cannot help but notice the many fudge shops located everywhere, souvenir T-shirt shops and ferries back and forth to Mackinac Island. Opting for the hot dog but passing on the fudge and ferry, I sat in the town center, bike close by, and soaked up the sun's rays. It had been a few days since

World's largest hot dog

I felt the sun's warmth on my face, and I was going to take my time
and enjoy.

To get across the bridge with a bike, your only option really is to
contact the Mackinac Bridge Authority for a lift. They do not allow
cyclists to ride across. In fact, the pedestrian walkway is so narrow,
it would be impossible to ride across. They advertise a phone number to call once you are in town. I first called just outside of town,
apparently breaking the rules, being told "call us when you are at
the hut." Okay. Will do. I am so sorry.

That is when I decided to chill, take my time, and grab one of
Wienerlicious' Chicago-style hot dogs. After the Chicago-style,
which was more like a distant suburb-of-Chicago-style hot dog than
the real thing, and in view of the hut, I called again.

"Are you <u>at</u> the hut?" I was asked.

"I am two blocks away," I replied.

"Call us when you are <u>at</u> the hut."

"Um, I can see it," I said meekly, as the authority hung up.

Thirty seconds later, with my left hand firmly and obediently
leaning against the wall of the hut, I called one more time.

"A transport should be there momentarily," the pleasant recep-
tionist relayed, then immediately hung up.

Progress. I had visions of an excursion van, possibly with bike
racks on the back, and comfortable seats to relax in, with the hope
to snap a few pictures as I traveled across the majestic bridge.

I waited for 15 minutes, then 20, then 25 minutes. I really did not
want to call this lovely individual on the other end of the phone
again for the fourth time so I just sat, taking her word that eventually
someone or something would show up. Finally, a rusty, old, black
pickup pulled up. If we were further south, the U.S. Border Patrol
would take one look at this pickup and assume it is a member of the
El Chapo Sinaloa Cartel, smuggling innocents across the border.
This was my $15 transportation across the bridge.

"Throw it in the back," Kyle ordered, as if it was a sack of potatoes.
He was talking about my treasured mount. He just stuck a knife in
my heart in our first 15 seconds together. It was not a great start.

"Throw it in the back?" I inquired, curious as to where and how. "Do you have any way to tie it up or secure it?"

"Just hop up there and lean it to the side," is all I got.

Now Kyle was half my age, a former third-string high school offensive lineman, I guessed, by his large size and his total indifference, but he was pissing me off. This beautiful display of engineering excellence that had transported me for more than 450 miles up to this point was being treated like a bag of garbage, and so was I.

"Relax, relax," I said to myself, "I need to get across." I finally convinced Kyle to assist me in the hopping, lifting and securing department, locking in the bike the best I could by leveraging old crates, orange construction cones and random pieces of cardboard scattered in the pickup's bed against the bike's frame. Minimally satisfied as to my bike's status, hopping down I took a quick glance at the passenger seat and could not help but notice that the seat was covered by "stuff," old coffee cups, McDonald's wrappers, papers and random garbage of all shapes and sizes.

"Um, where should I sit?" I asked politely.

Without saying a word, Kyle reached out his right arm and with one waving motion, pushed the pile of trash to the floor. Problem solved. We were on our way.

Immediately, it was evident that I was not my friend's sole focus of attention at that moment. In addition to me, we were on official duty also escorting a huge semi carrying an immense construction crane as it attempted to cross the bridge. I was an odd lot and an inconvenience to his bigger, better-paying mission. We drove right behind this immense tractor trailer, emergency lights flashing, traveling half the speed of the other cars and trucks in the lane to my left. I could not see anything. Apart from looking straight to my right, my view was completely blocked. My vision of comfort and grand views of beautiful blue waters, islands and historic lighthouses as I crossed the bridge, was not exactly playing out as planned. Comfort, nope. View, nada. Conversation, forget about it.

"Do you do this service often for bikers?" I asked, attempting to engage.

"I think I had a cyclist last month, can't remember," I got back. More silence. I quickly attempted a selfie of me, and my bike, it leaning hard to starboard in the pickup's bed, as proof that it was really there, as I envisioned that call to my insurance guy, explaining how my bike, unsecured, bounced out of the pickup bed and off the Mackinac Bridge, lost forever.

More silence.

Sitting there with little else in the way of entertainment, my thoughts wandered back to years before on a memorable sailing trip, and the sail under this very bridge. Our trip took us north from Beaver Island with my buddy and our collective five kids, aged 12 to 16. We were pressing to get to Mackinac Island in order to secure one of the last remaining slips before they filled for the day.

The winds had picked up and were consistently over 20 knots out of the south. As we turned to our right, and east, we passed under the bridge on a broad reach, heeling to port, with all five of the junior-sailors life-jacketed up and on the starboard rail, offering counterbalance. It is a memory each of us still carries to this day. Today's bridge adventure with blocked view and ankle deep in discarded McDonald's wrappers was not as scintillating.

Finally arriving across the Bridge, we pulled over to the side of Interstate 75, the Trek Terror amazingly still intact. Fifteen dollars lighter, I built up the nerve to ask, "Do you know how I get into town?"

"Nope." Silence.

"I think there might be a bike path over there somewhere," is what I got back. Kyle, always so generous, pointed toward the woods, no path in sight. His indifference was overwhelming.

Thanking Kyle for his services, nonetheless, I rode off in search of a bike path or some semblance of a rideable road not named I-75, that would take me into St. Ignace. There was no bike path. There was no foot path. There was no rideable road. Google Maps was confused. Garmin, as a tease, offered me a route. It looked like I would have to scurry across I-75, as those semis and other menaces came flying off the bridge.

Garmin then pointed me to a gravel road that, first, took me under

My other "transportation" for the day

the interstate, but ultimately into town. I hate gravel roads, but I was out of options. I gave it a try. Riding on dirt, tackling one more short, steep hill for fun's sake and my mission was finally accomplished. I found St. Ignace! My bike was okay. I was okay. I was finally in the Upper Peninsula!

St. Ignace is a historian's dream, situated in the far most eastern part of the Upper Peninsula of Michigan. The famed Father Marquette had his mission here and the Ojibwas, one of the area's predominant Native American tribal populations, had their museum. Marquette established Michigan's earliest European settlement, living among the Great Lakes Indians from 1666 to his death in 1675. The irony and synergy of one's mission turning into someone else's museum kind of caught me.

Three hundred years ago this was a different place than today as French explorers were in search of The Great Water, the river they believed led to the Pacific Ocean, and St. Ignace was their hangout. The Ojibwa, which translates into "the original people," together with the Chippewa and Potawatomi, controlled large swaths of the upper Midwest that encompassed the lands around Lake Superior and Lake Michigan. They were continually pushed westward, seldom by choice. St. Ignace is where Lake Michigan and Lake Huron meet in the Straits of Mackinac, and the five-mile-long Mackinac Bridge connects north and south between the Upper Peninsula and the rest of Michigan.

The waters are like a witch's cauldron and the winds are typically strong, often gale-force. Most travelers heading across the bridge and into the UP, as locals call it, fly right past St. Ignace on the way to somewhere else. Besides the tourist ferries running back and forth to Mackinac Island, there is not much going on. Yet here I was on a bike, already up the entire west coast of Michigan, through northern Michigan and over the bridge, and I needed a place to stay.

Like most towns so far, my housing choices were limited. My list of criteria prioritized starting with location and if they have a shower, and then free breakfast and a working TV. Allowing the bike in the room was a luxury, for most motel managers barely even looked up, let alone gave me the once over, so that was somewhat automatic. Since I was on a bike, putting my bike in my room was kind of important, as well as location because unnecessary pedaling was silly, so I always wanted an easy in and out of town, thus location and the bike in the room. I rarely asked about the latter. A shower speaks for itself, as does a free breakfast. Free and unlimited food prior to a day's ride is crucial, but not always possible. The cost issue as it relates to motels is a matter of splitting hairs, since they tend to all be in the same cost zip code.

Mentally throwing darts, I settled on the Driftwood Motel. It looked better than most and bragged about its "'Legendary' Mighty Mac Burger." Mighty Mac is the locals' nickname for the bridge. Below this declaration, though, on the sign, as if it is not related or relevant, they highlight they need line cooks. Plural. Hmmm. With that in mind, I decided simple and easy was the way to go. I chose the whitefish sandwich. You never quite know what is in the whitefish, but the local couple sitting next to me, who knew Crystal behind the bar by name, had it and they looked no worse for the wear. Smothered with tartar sauce, astride a generous plateful of home-made fries, they hit the spot.

Finally, I was off to find the Mission, or at least the Museum. Both were closed. No real reason as to why, just closed. Knowing I had to hit the road early the next morning, option three was triggered when I walked past a Dollar General and decided to go in. My Beats earbuds got fried two days earlier in a monsoon on the way to Traverse City and I was hoping to find a replacement. Not expecting Dollar General to have anything remotely representing post-Millennium technology, let alone something with their own logo, I surprisingly found the answer staring right at me as I walked in. Right past the front door, hanging on a rack were the DG wireless ear buds for $19. One set was left! I was saved.

Checking out, the kid behind the counter said, "$9." I replied, "Really, $9?" He said "Yeah, on sale."

Right, Dollar General. I wish they had 14 more.

Dinner done, St. Ignace sightseeing finished before it started, earbuds in tow, I was ready to crash. The room was like most I had stayed in, possibly nicer. Overdone in that logger motif, it looked like the last full renovation was possibly back before the Nixon administration, but it was comfortable enough, located on the main strip and across from the harbor. Maybe I would even get a free sunrise as I was leaving in the morning. The plan was to push all the way to Manistique, 90 plus miles to the west, and then 75 more the next day to Escanaba, and I knew I had little margin for error given roads, wind and likely rain.

Line cooks. Plural.

DAY NINE

The UP

My route setting out appeared longer than the 90-plus A-to-B route along Lake Michigan I had hoped for. Garmin had suggested avoiding Highway 2 and traveling on smaller roads, so I knew I had a full day. Traveling the back roads, Garmin estimated that I would travel 105 miles, maybe 110, before the day was done. There was not much margin for error or hiccups. If something happened to my bike or me over this stretch there were few choices of places to stop for the night.

The morning ritual was the same. Get up pre-dawn; check the weather, specifically for temperature, wind, wind direction and the likelihood of rain; and organize accordingly. Rain, wind, and cold are the three biggest influencers to the quality of the day. At some point, given the three influencers, you are forced to come inside to warm up and dry off. Miles are impacted. Unplanned minutes push back arrival time.

Up to that point, due to the influencer of rain, my motel rooms have ended up looking like a yard sale with clothing hung everywhere possible or spread across heating vents to dry. Shoes, gloves, helmet, riding pants, everything. I have used motel hair dryers four times so far and never once for my hair. Rain impacts everything.

The next task was coffee. I must have coffee. The stronger the better. Then food, ideally the type that fills you up like bacon and eggs, cereal, and toast, but that takes too long most days, so you settle. Starting out, I inhaled a bad gas station powdered-sugar donut that was probably still there when the building was converted from a

White Hen into this BP station six years earlier, and a large burnt coffee that gas stations own the patent on. But I did not care. I had to hit the road.

Water bottles filled, panniers repacked in reverse order of need with rain jacket and RXBARs on top, tires checked one more time, hopeful destination plugged into both Garmin GPS and Google Maps, highlighting my insecure opinion of both, it was *"go time!"*

It is amazing. Once pedaling, you feel younger. Your age difference between that first foot on the floor pre-dawn, and five miles into the ride feels like two generations of aging have dropped right off. Every day.

That morning, the air was dry and crisp, so crisp that fog was rising off the bogs to either side as I rode, casting crazy sorcerous shadows as they heated up. It felt like it was in the mid-40s. My Garmin, just to argue, said it was 50. Heading west, the rising orange sun off the lake, behind me to the east, projected my shadow before I got there. I liked what I saw. My hands tight on the aerobars, body streamlined, legs pumping, my $9 earbuds were cooperating, throwing off Creedence, The Boss, Allman Brothers and Mick as needed to match each peddle push. The two-lane road was straight, fairly smooth and empty.

Snapping my beautiful Zen moment, I heard across my new earbuds, "In 600 feet take a right, on Crossbow Trail."

"Wait, what? That can't be. I mapped it out this morning."

"Karen" from Garmin repeated herself, saying "At the next intersection take a right." When I got there, all I could see was a dirt road, with potholes and rocks for as far as the eye could see. This path would love nothing more than to make my skinny tires not as skinny anymore.

I said out loud "Nope, not happening."

Continuing past the impolite interruption to my now-playing Stones montage, I barreled down the road. For the next four miles, my personal selection of life's greatest rock and roll was repeatedly interrupted by "Karen," recommending I leave this smooth, hard asphalt, to jump on to that dreaded mine field of Crossbow Trail, which appeared to be running parallel. The earbuds came off.

Enough.

I went back to attacking the rolling hills, imagining a couple of young 20-somethings penned up inside a small room in Garmin's headquarters, laughing to themselves about how today they were really going to ruin some older cyclist's day. I showed them. Not today.

Suddenly, there it was. Right in front of me was that warned-off Highway 2! This highway was not any typical two-, sometimes four-lane highway. It starts out in the Pacific Northwest, somewhere in central Washington state, passing through the Bitterroot Mountain Range in Idaho and Montana, zigging and zagging into North Dakota and Minnesota, until it hits the northern most rocky shores of Lake Michigan, where it runs along the southern shoreline of the Upper Peninsula of Michigan and continues east into St. Ignace, where land becomes sea. I had been warned off Route 2 by a couple of cyclists I

Route 2 heaven

had encountered earlier, as well as my Garmin pal, and was dreading the additional 15-20 miles recommended by Garmin.

I was shocked. The road looked perfect. New asphalt, wide shoulders and relatively flat. A cyclist's dream. I could not believe it. "Trust your instincts. Make your own assessment." Time to crush, and I got after it.

The wind was light but favorable, kissing my right shoulder with a subtle push. On my left, as far as the eyes could see, was the sandy and rocky shore of the lake Native Americans called Michigami. Tall dune grasses waved a welcoming wave, as if they had been waiting for me.

The shoreline glistened with glacier strewn boulders interrupting its mirror, and the water was as clear as anywhere on earth. On my right was an endless canopy of native tall growth pine, maple and oak. I could get used to this. These are the days, as a cyclist, you live for, smooth roads, lively legs, favorable wind and amazing scenery.

It is not a straight shot to Manistique. There are drive-through hamlets and petrol stopovers on the way named Brevort, Naubinway, Gould City and Gulliver, which collectively might equal a small town but offer little besides a gas station, gas station store and a town diner that is just barely hanging on. If you need a place to stay you might be sleeping in your car. I have no car. I have no tent, for that matter. Weight is weight, after all.

Entering each hamlet, one can see many buildings, but a lot are empty, boarded-up remnants of time past. The number of abandoned motels is most striking. Most have been abandoned for a while, certainly well before the Pandemic excuse, and just lie in wait, as the national forest's never-ending creep attempts to reclaim them back into their fold. An occasional auto repair shop pops up from time to time, but the few cars and pickups in front tell you even this business has seen better days.

Without the need, nor desire, for anything remotely imitating a red light, or warning yellow in these towns to slow things down, traffic rumbles by.

The ride was solid, making good time, but I was getting that first nudge after 30 or 35 miles to take five. It is amazing how those few seconds allow you to recharge the hands, small of the back and legs. Your hands grow numb from the constant pressure on the handlebars. I have aerobars which extend forward off my handlebars, resting my elbows and adding a different grip with my hands. What a difference those make, but it still takes a toll on your hands. The back and legs love variety, as well, so a constant, flat surface, though appreciated, takes a toll. You are constantly, although unconsciously, taking body parts inventory as the ride progresses. Hands, neck, lower back, hammies, all good? Good.

Often, you scout possible destinations and potential stops but lock in nothing. This is the joy of riding. You stop based on fatigue, hunger or something interesting. This time I pulled over for something interesting. To my left, in one of the many national forests, this time the Hiawatha National Forest, was a scenic overhang looking out at the beautiful waters of the great lake and beyond. Being situated higher up above the shoreline, the view begs for that, soon-to-be-ignored, iPhone photo that seldom turns out in the same image as what you see with your own eyes right in front of you. Despite being on the road for nine days, the view still takes your breath away, and that is what you remember.

The golden, sandy beaches and dune grass slowly transitioned to sediment, rock and boulders from millions of years ago until the glistening lake wins the battle between water and earth. The nearby waters eventually drop off to depths of close to 900 feet. They may be called "the Great Lakes," but they are inland seas dumping from west-to-east in a slow-motion river, with each lake dumping like a bucket into the lake east of them until it reaches the St. Lawrence River. It begins with Lake Superior at the head waters, then Michigan and Huron combined, as they are just one giant lake, then Erie and Ontario, dropping into the St. Lawrence River, and ultimately into the Atlantic Ocean.

On this day, the lake was stunning, somewhat calm and showing off its colors, from green to blue and every color in between. Straight out, maybe 20 miles you could see the nubs of Beaver Island, Hog Island and Garden Island. Beaver Island is the largest island in Lake Michigan and has a history that Dickens could not make up.

As I mentioned when traveling earlier through Charlevoix, the island became the theocracy and monarchy of one King James Strang, who lost the coin flip to Brigham Young for leadership of the Mormon Church. Young went west as head of the Latter-day Saints, Strang stayed on Beaver Island with his small band of loyalists. He and his tribe, the Strangites, a name more conducive to a heavy metal band than a religious organization, were subsequently wiped out soon after the split under mysterious circumstances. It could have been one of his five wives. The island was eventually retaken by the previously dispossessed American fishermen who had settled in Beaver Island from County Donegal, Ireland, years earlier.

Flashing back to years ago, I had the fortune to stop at Beaver Island on my way sailing to Mackinac Island. Little pops up as memorable besides a certain, distinctive sulphur smell covering the entire island, a breakfast diner that was not that bad and mayflies, lots and lots of mayflies. If unfamiliar, mayflies are nasty looking flying insects that are typically three to four inches long with a heritage that goes all the way back prior to the dinosaurs and looks more appropriate for the Amazon than northern Lake Michigan.

What is amazing is that these swarms have a lifespan of only a couple of days, so when we saw them, they were definitely on a mission. They were so plentiful that I had to reach my hand through six inches of mayfly-swarming thickness just to open the diner's screen door. That memory stayed with my teenager crowd for days afterwards. After a quick sunrise meal, we could not hop back on our sailboat and split this insect-laden island fast enough.

As my thoughts transitioned to those 600 or so citizens who cast their lot full time on such a stark yet remarkable island, and their myriad reasons as to why they chose to hide out here, I knew it was time once again for me to move on and hit the road.

The road at 16 to 17 mph gives you the freedom driving at 70 does not allow. At 70, you must be somewhere. Not as much at my speed.

You notice things, most of which your mind forgets 10 minutes later under the last-in-first-out rule. But occasionally those thoughts stay with you until something even more interesting nudges them aside. There are the signs for the always present national forests, state parks, national lakeshores, state lakeshores, scenic lookouts, and those vestiges themselves that warrant such signs. These keep you engaged.

Then you have the billboards, not as numerous as I-94 driving through Gary but out there, nonetheless. A lot of the signs speak about churches of this ilk or that, inviting you in with promised redemption, but the sign for the Kewadin Casino, located 50 miles down the road, caught my eye. Granted, 50 miles by car is faster than by bike, but you wonder why here? Why is this sign in the middle of a national forest, on a lone stretch of Highway 2 and miles away from anywhere, let alone 50 miles from Manistique.

Given what I had seen so far, and the underwhelming array of interesting human-made things, I must assume 99 percent of the people who live up here already know what and where it is. For the one percent driving through, and the .01 percent of those that might react positively to such signage, I guess it is enlightening but, I repeat, why there?

It was at this moment I realized the sign worked.

This is what goes through your head while pedaling for miles. That is until your stomach slaps aside your message machine upstairs and starts saying, *"I'm the captain, now,"* or something along those lines. Time for lunch!

As you may have guessed, food options, if you wish to call them that, along Highway 2 are limited. Stopping in Naubinway, a little more than half my day's journey, gave me two options. The first was a diner that would fit right into a Stephen King novel. Even with my bike just feet from the front door, I was unclear whether the place was even open. The only giveaway was the one car parked in front, but even that is not definite, given the car's age, rust and overall condition. It could have been left here and abandoned years ago.

I decided to check out option two, the gas station store. It is always interesting the looks one gets when walking into any place wearing cycling garb, but it is especially true when cycling through the Upper Peninsula. The strange cycling pants and jersey; the fluorescent yellow jacket that is much more appropriate for hunting days up here than cycling; and the weird bike helmet, glasses and biking shoes with their pedal clips that make you walk funny; make one slightly stand out from the crowd. You get stares. Yet the store people are nice enough and point me to the sliding glassed-door refrigerator. My choices are ham and cheese and cheese and ham, both on white bread. Or I could go back to the Stephen King next door. It looked like I should choose ham and cheese.

I flashed back to an image from a couple of weeks earlier and the food-brewery emporium I was in, highlighted by my "Elvis Has Left the Beer Church" sandwich consisting of peanut butter, jelly, bananas and bacon on a toasted roll, a cyclist's dream, mind you. I could only dream fondly. This was a different story. Sandwich in hand, I purposely did not even attempt to look at expiration dates stamped on the non-feast, fearful that the answer may force me toward a second visit to The Shining next door.

It was not bad.

Walking out, hydrated, legs rested and satisfied that the food would stay down, I took one last glance at the option one next door, which looked exactly the same as before with the one car in front, and I retook the road.

I think a lot about all those people up there, their lives, and who may have lived there before, in better days. Each of those empty buildings has a story. The UP has a toughness to it. It could be the knowing that winter is not far away which means feet and feet of snow off Lakes Superior and Michigan, strong winds and frigid cold. This is why God invented the snowmobile, Budweiser and cannabis, I guess.

Nature, though, has a way of offering a peace pipe of sorts in advance of those months of dread by producing stunning arrays of color, reds and oranges and yellows, before the trees lay bare for the next six months. The colors are their reward for their hardships and mine. The palettes of color are just emerging, welcoming me. This toughness could also be the general understanding that one is on their own. Self-sufficiency is the rule. Knowing the success or failure of one's day is up to them, their hard work, grit and ingenuity, not some bureaucrats in Washington, makes one tough. This adds an edge that is hard to miss.

There is another thing I noticed. By their nature, whether pure suspicion of outsiders or Norwegian roots, they do not start conversations. If one was not started, the room would be silent, but if you make a statement or ask a question, they could not be more helpful. I found this many times, whether it was asking directions, commenting on the weather or asking which gas station between Naubinway and Gould City had the better ham sandwich.

A final observation: I am not sure who this Brandon guy is, or where he is going, but he seemed to be popular in the UP. There are signs everywhere wishing him well in the form of "Let's Go!" it would seem. It could be that independent voice I see and hear so much up here.

Once again, my Dollar General $9's in my ears, cranking Dylan and then John Prine back-to-back, I continued to make good time. Kind of out of the blue, just past Naubinway and still on Highway 2, I stopped at the entrance to the GarLyn Zoo Wildlife Park. A zoo in the middle of nowhere, literally, was created by Gary and Lynn if you hadn't already figured it out by the name. Their claim is that they are the largest zoo in the eastern Upper Peninsula, but I would guess that is a rather small sample size of one.

They started by raising potbellied pigs, pygmy goats and peacocks. They were forced into selling their truck to pay for the animals' food, but eventually the zoo caught on and today it includes tigers, lions, a bear of some sort, bison, hyenas and tortoises. I can only think about how these savanna natives enjoy the nine months not called summer. Plus, the idea that a caged-in zoo exists in the middle of 16,000 square miles of other animals not caged up in

The "other" Bates Motel

the UP, seems interesting. I wanted to stop and check it out, but I knew this would not be a 15-minute stop and I had a deadline in Manistique.

Heading through Gould City, 15 miles past the zoo, and 30 still to reach Manistique, I was struck by the sight of a single motel and had to stop. It was not just any motel but the Bates Motel. It looked as you would expect and hope, decrepit, light flickering on and off, another one where you were uncertain as to its status. As part of the Bates Motel sign out in front you got no further help. The flickering lighted sign reported "No Vacancy" while the hand-lettered after-thought sign, attached and to its right, said "Vacancy." Beautiful. One would hope this was created by one entrepreneur with a flair for the macabre, but life is simpler.

This motel was bought earlier in the year by one Theresa Bates, who thought it was cute, claiming she did not watch TV and had never heard of the movie nor the Bates Motel. Once the woman issuing the motel license and other people kept bringing up the "other one," she decided to watch the movie and, making lemonade out of lemons, embraced the horror theme and created one room appropriately named "Psycho," with the mandatory bloody footprints and handprints throughout the room, and other such ghoulish things. It is reported that the Psycho Room is their most popular room of all, despite the added surcharge up to the steep price of $75, instead of the standard $50. I passed. I would use the 30 miles to Manistique as my excuse.

When motivated, I can ride hard. Knowing I had just under 30 miles to go and wanting to put Psycho in the rearview mirror, I pushed onward. During one of my leg-stretch, hydration stops, I inhaled a Snickers bar and researched my choices for accommodations for the evening. Again, my priorities started with close location in and out of town, meaning street and first floor (mandatory), then working shower, closeness to something edible, closeness to something with beer in the name, free coffee, free breakfast, and hopefully, bike in the room. My demands were growing by the day. Cost could float from first to last based on visuals.

It is interesting, when one starts to share pictures and/or descriptions of current or past accommodations with loved ones, you tend to get "opinions" back. Most start with, "I can't believe you stayed there!" and go rapidly downhill from there. I find staying at motels offers charm and a slice of Americana. You cannot help but meet interesting people. After all, what are your real needs? A shower, working TV, a night's sleep, an A/C unit actually working relatively quietly and and a place to clean off and repack your bike. Simple. Occasionally, my soul weakened, and I opted for that multi-floor and elevatored, breakfast-included, hot-tubbed slice of an upgrade, but after that one night of a comfortable sleep and full breakfast I got back on the horse I rode in on.

Again, my choices were limited. I settled for the Harbor View Motel. Nice name. As I rode up, I noticed it really was not by the harbor, nor really any body of water for that matter. Its view is of a former tool and dye factory that appears to have closed sometime during the Vietnam War, but I was sure it would be fine. After 90 miles and several hours in the saddle, all I really wanted was a hot shower, ample food and a beer.

I knocked on the office door, which was locked, and then I saw the sign "Don't knock. Press the buzzer." I was already in the land of Oz, starting on the wrong foot. I wondered if the wizard was home. After much too long, Nick from the Harbor View Motel answered the door, and said, "What!?" It was not a "What" with a smile and a twinkle in the eye. He obviously lived in a room behind the office based on his appearance, and I felt like I had just interrupted something important. Nonetheless, I explained my desire to secure a night in his lovely establishment and we were heading in the right direction.

Key secured and location determined, a couple of things struck me right away. First, I had seen when researching that there was a brewery in town, so I asked my pal Nick about its whereabouts. Shoulder shrug. He had no idea. Upon which, I happened to glance across the street–literally across the street–to see the Flatiron Brewing Company. Given his demeanor and urgency to get back to whatever he was doing, I kept my reaction to myself.

My second observation was, entering my room, there were two hand printed signs, both the same wording but clearly done at different times, one on top of the other, stating, "Absolutely NO marijuana in the Room!!!" I kind of understood the one sign, despite pot legality in the state of Michigan, as a courtesy to patrons. But the second one, underneath the first, interested me.

Were we really in the Land of Oz and the lower one was for the Munchkins when they came to visit? I never got my answer. I did not care, I was on a mission, because all I wanted was to take a shower and hit the brewery. After a full day of riding, all you want to do is remove those filthy bike clothes and jump in the shower.

Which I started to do. Stark-ass naked, shower blasting, I noticed my 18-inch-wide by 18-inch-deep folding-door shower, the size of which half of the people I know on earth could not fit into, is refusing to warm up. I waited and waited. So, my Harbor View Motel had neither a harbor view nor hot water. Great. I knew I must call Nick from Oz about the water, but I really, really, really didn't want to call Nick. After another too-long wait, me standing in a towel, Nick answered the phone and said, "What?" Again, with that voice.

I politely explained my predicament and he said he would be "right over," which meant him going to the water heater room next to my room and adjusting things. That was not what I thought it might be, which included Nick barging into my room, me stark-ass naked, and, ahem, adjusting things. I was relieved it was the former.

The water problem solved, me freshly scrubbed, I knew my next destination. Flatiron! It was located between my motel and the actual harbor, with the Manistique Lighthouse a similar distance out in the water. It was small but cute, with a great setting and I was ready. The brewery looked newer, with fresh, decorative wood outside and inside, and a nice bar with multiple taps of local and homemade brew.

The setting had a lonesome feel, as it sat on the edge of a small, sparsely filled harbor. Post-Labor Day explained some of the reasons for the many open slips but not all. Undeterred, I walked in, curious and thirsty. Marina, yes, Marina, the bartender, and the entire staff for that matter, greeted me with a smile and I bellied up to the bar. Settling on the recommended Doppelbock, I was in heaven. Although I was the only human being, besides Marina, in the place, it was perfect, with Marina playing a Jimmy Buffett tribute in the background celebrating his recent passing and pouring me the tastiest of dark beer. The universe was aligned once again.

There is something magical when you bring a long day of exercise to its conclusion and add great music and a good beer. Cyclists know this more than most. That is why they have plentiful of both at the end of so many multi-day rides. It brings things together in a tight circle of contentment, knowing that although you did not split the atom, or solve global warming, you made a positive step forward.

The first D-Bock immediately emptied, I ordered a second, all the time talking about the ride, what I saw along the route, the rain heading our way, and whereabouts of good food. Marina seemed fairly interested in all things related to the ride and was most helpful on the food part. Tap 21 was her endorsement, "best burger in town." I was relieved to note there was no comment about the need for line cooks. Plus, it was close to my castle for the night, my Harbor View Motel. No need to phone a friend or get a second opinion. This was the ticket.

Tap 21 was as advertised. The hamburger was massive and did the job. The beer hit the spot. Satisfied in multiple ways with food and drink, I finally headed to the motel, looking forward to watching some college football, getting reorganized and ultimately, some shut-eye, knowing the next day's weather prospects looked iffy, at best. Getting organized becomes second nature after nine days, but still takes thought. Hot or cold? Rain or shine? Places to stop for water, food? Tools, tubes, bike wrenches? Google and Garmin charged? Ear buds charged? Check, check, check, check.

Attempting to twist the universe by doing two things at the same time, and it being Saturday, I also tried to find the college football games on the channel changer. By this time, you may have guessed that this is not the Four Seasons. I don't think this would qualify for even One Season, maybe more like that period in late February, early March that everyone hates, but I was still hopeful. The room still had a bed, a TV of some sort and a shower for anorexics. Plus, of course, a filthy, grungy road bike with skinny tires and saddle bags caked with the day's road grunge parked between the door and the bed.

I was a little perplexed, though, by the white duct tape on the back of the TV remote and handwritten lettering announcing "ON-OFF." Is this an Upper Peninsula Mensa test? Is there a camera recording this? Despite the lane change, I flipped over the remote, hit the red button and on it came. Yes! Sensing progress, I proceeded to hit one, then multiple buttons, to no avail.

No matter what pounding and whacking I did, the channel would not change. The channel on my TV screen was fixed on the Hallmark Channel, in the middle of some 1983 murder-mystery classic, as far as I could tell, and no matter what I did or hit, on the remote or the TV itself, Hallmark won, and I lost. College football was not going to happen. Deciding that calling Mr. Harbor View Motel past 8 p.m. would not work out to my advantage, I finished my organizing, bid Hallmark a good night, and hit the hay, dreams of college football in my head.

The Land of Oz

DAY 10

Guardian Angels

Still dark and clearly not morning, I woke up to a sound like popcorn popping, not the smell, just the sound. I had heard this sound before, previously on this ride and on other rides. I knew this sound. It's not popcorn, it's you-know-what. There are a few words, only a select few, that one never utters out loud while on a bike trip. One is "F-l-a-t," and the other is "R-a-i-n." I hear the "R" word, and those drops sounded big. I rolled over and closed my eyes.

At some point, the inevitable became evitable. You know that the rain is supposed to last all day, and you know you must get out of bed. You have that feeling like the day your dog died, maybe not as sad, but a gray pale, nonetheless. Added to that, my One Season of Oz motel failed to add "coffee" to its list of "must-haves" for the visitor's total satisfaction, so I moved one notch higher on the grumpy meter.

There are times, moments, when one is faced with two opposing spirits, the former being that of Knute Rockne, the legendary Notre Dame football coach, and the other being Sluggo the Sloth. The former spirit instills positive, actionable, connective energy, as your mind tells you to "GO! GO! GO!" while the latter, well, the opposite. I rallied my best Knute, got dressed—layer after layer, rain gear on top—put on my ear buds with "Cheeseburger in Paradise" blasting in both ears, took one last glance in the mirror framing my bike and me, the image punctuating my bright yellow, and said to no one in particular, "Go time!" I rolled my bike out the door and into the cold rain.

Tires rolling on the wet pavement, I noticed it was obviously not "Go time" for the rest of civilization as I was the only human being in sight. No cars, no walkers and certainly no other cyclists. Granted, it was just past sunrise, the sun totally blocked out by the thick clouds overhead, but where was everyone? Undeterred, I was pumped. More road for me!

Making one quick stop at the Marathon for a small dark coffee and last week's freshest, I hit the road. As I left Manistique, the rain was a mist, but it picked up like it needed to be somewhere. Hoping not to be marginalized by the rain, the winds did their best to have their say. Originating from somewhere in the Rockies, flying across the Dakotas and the upper Midwest, they smacked me in the face like they meant it. Wind and rain. Wind and rain. My next stop was Escanaba, still in Michigan and still in the Upper Peninsula, but the distance felt a lot longer. In real miles, it was not as far as the 90-mile day the day before, still cruising Highway 2. But given the conditions, it felt close. I was expecting a similar road surface, and shoulders, but I knew the day would be challenging.

It's interesting how your knees and hips respond when riding in the cold, pouring rain versus the warm sunshine. It is more like a chipmunk sticking its nose outside its burrow, fearful of the hawk overhead, not sure if it wants to totally commit. That is how my hips and knees responded—an "I'll get back to you, Gene," from "Apollo 13" kind of thing.

In warmth and sunshine, everything jump-starts around the same time, ready to go and fully engaged at two or three miles down the road. In cold and rain, the machine parts, the knees, back, hips and hands, submit to the inevitable, but individually, like school kids looking at each other for assurance.

Escanaba has a long history of logging, fishing and hunting. Some of this is ancient history but there are still things to see. You have the Escanaba River, the Escanaba Harbor, and the Sand Point Lighthouse. I didn't try this, given the stream of rain hitting me in the face, but I would venture that one could walk from the river to the harbor to the lighthouse and back, and still have time for a pint at the Upper Hand Brewery, where Deer Camp and Yooper Ale are popular.

A point of pride in town is the Jeff Daniels' 2001 comedy "Escanaba in da Moonlight." Shot in Escanaba, it was surprisingly shut out when that year's Oscar nominations were announced. An Upper Peninsula classic centered around hunting and drinking, its most memorable line was "Escanaba is like Christmas with guns!" I would guess there are still copies available in the last remaining Blockbuster store, outside Bend, Oregon, but you better hurry.

Getting ahead of myself, the wet road unfolded in front of me, and the miles ticked off. In the rain, especially cold rain, your hands go numb first. You can move them around, from handlebars, to aerobars, to lower handlebar drops, and then back again, but they still go numb. You do whatever you can do to get blood back in the fingers.

Eventually, though, you need to find a place to stop, preferably someplace warm and dry. There was such a place 30-some miles down the road, a Marathon station, looking somewhat warm and dry. Google Maps reported this was my only real option for the next 20 miles. Time to stop.

I generally find the men and women behind the counter of these prairie stop-over fueling stations to be usually nice and in a good mood. Consistently, as I walked into the stores of these places of petrol, I was greeted by a smile and an anxiousness to be of assistance. I never really figured out why. It could have been my desperate appearance in my rain-soaked, mud-splattered outfit, but I'm going with the idea that those people are just nice folks. Being from the large city, I have found nice, smiley people always made me put a firmer grip on my wallet, not that I even knew where in my panniers my wallet was at that moment.

In that specific Marathon station, it was time for a hot cup of coffee and a Snickers bar. The time for these two simple tasks takes longer than it should or would on a dry, 80-degree day, but no fault lied with my cheery compatriots behind the counter. It was all about the rain and cold. I savored each warm sip and Snickers nourishment, to the last bite. Watching the rain hammer everything in sight, I stalled until I could stall no longer. I headed back outside, grabbed my handlebars, raised my right leg and rode off.

I was back in the same movie—wind, rain, cold, wind, rain, cold. Semis and pickups hummed past to my near left and still separated by the lone rumble strip. Considering everything, I felt pretty good. All parts of me were synchronized and cooperating. You know it will be the cold that eventually gets you, but you block those thoughts toward better vibes.

More random thoughts popped up in my head. Since traveling through mid-Michigan, and especially in northern Michigan and the UP, you see a lot of days-gone-by, empty, boarded-up buildings and the like, but what stood out over the past several days was that every shiny new building seemed to be a cannabis dispensary. Lots and lots of cannabis dispensaries, and they were beautiful, modernistic and inviting.

I passed stores named "Glazed and Confused," "Lume," "77 North," "Elevated Exotics," "The Fire Station," "Wacky Jackz," "Dunegrass" and "Cloud Cannabis." There were many more, but you get the idea. Add in the infused farm-to-table spots, harvest-rally spots and medical centers, and you know things are going on. I understand the demand. Have you ever spent a winter month in the Upper Peninsula? Me neither, but I imagine, come January and February, one is itching for some recreational activity not requiring 30 pounds of goose feathers, heavy winter boots and goggles.

It's the supply that was surprising. These were well-designed, well-funded buildings that someone was making a big bet on. Couple all of that with the fact that these were all located in a part of the United States that averages 18 souls per square mile, I repeat, something interesting is going on.

A second observation, and I may stretch and say the two observations have a unique cause-and-effect relationship, were all the food joints of the same ilk. It occurred to me that if a space alien happened to land in the UP, they would assume that our total sustenance consisted of BBQ and Taco Tuesday. Everywhere you go, the town could have only one place to eat, a breakfast place at that, yet they would offer BBQ and Taco Tuesday. Cause and effect are in play.

With rain in my eyes, and pretty much everywhere else, and no signs of letting up, I had food on my mind. With 50 miles behind me for the day, I stopped for lunch. I saw Joe's Eats' neon sign a mile up the road and figured it was a sign of a different kind. I parked my bike against their side wall, ducked my helmeted head to the stream of rainwater cascading off the roofed overhang, and walked in, or attempted to. The place was packed, totally packed.

The diner was exactly as you would expect up there: a small counter with five stools, so popular back in the '50s, and one large room with approximately 15 tables, waitresses scurrying back and forth. I struck up a conversation with the head waitress, "Call me Q, Son" who pointed to the one seat still available at the counter, and I was set.

To do what I was attempting took a thicker skin than most, to say the least, but when you walk into a small-town diner for the first time, wearing bright fluorescence and absolutely soaked, and EVERYBODY in the place turns and stares in your direction, it is a little unnerving. My comment, "Hey 'Q,' this place is packed," resulted in the quick retort of "It's raining. Farmers got nothing to do," and off she went. I liked her immediately. I guessed her young Gen-Z junior waitresses maybe not so much.

Seat secured, monsoon outside, I took off the soaked bike helmet and fogged glasses and

Rain-splashed glasses

settled in. I was in no hurry. First it was hot coffee to warm myself, and water, which one could argue was redundant, given my last three plus hours. Then a bowl of cream of broccoli soup. Outstanding, and I was just beginning. Biscuits and gravy next, covering the entire plate. Looking outside, the rain continued to pound. I kept ordering off the menu, as much to delay the inevitable, as the fact that the food was amazingly good. Apple pie was next. You have to try the apple pie, right?

Finally, with no other choices to order and the day getting long, speaking in a sorrowful but reverential voice, I asked "Q" for the check.

"Here you go, son," "Q" said as she slapped the pink receipt in front of me. I kept my double take to myself as my bill was less than two grande four-adjective lattes at Clark and Division in Chicago. I thanked "Q," quickly paid, and once again hit the road.

Warmed up, belly full, I was set for the last 20-some miles to Escanaba. When you start getting close to your destination and have recently refueled, you get a charge, pushing your speed up another mile-per-hour or so, anticipating that shower, beer and meal. It was still raining, a little lighter, but with no sign of letting up.

I could taste the road grit as I rode. Spit from the tires connecting with the muddy shoulder created Howdy Doody freckles across the face and glasses, and the yellow raingear top had turned blackish in the middle of the back from top to bottom. I was constantly wiping each glass lens with my fingers, just to provide visibility. The rest of me? No worries. That is what showers are for. Approaching Escanaba, I started seeing signs of life. First billboards, then actual buildings.

Thoughts of Escanaba were in my head. Where to stay and eat? It was Sunday and the first week of the NFL season, and I knew football would be on TV in the bars and restaurants. There was great hope for my hometown Chicago Bears, and they were the highlighted late afternoon national game so I pedaled harder.

Just then, I got that feeling. It is hard to describe, but every cyclist unfortunately knows it. The feeling that something doesn't feel right. Looking down, first at the front tire, then the back, I sank. "No, not again."

My back tire, rock hard seconds earlier, was half as hard and headed to the point of no return. By the time I stopped it was a shadow of its former self. That "F" word. Six miles from Escanaba. I stopped off the shoulder, truck spray attacking from behind every few seconds as the rain picked up. I considered my options. One, I could move my bike further off the shoulder, on to the downward sloping prairie grass, amidst the spray and rain and mud, and change my tire. Or I could walk to find shelter. Looking down the road, a quarter of a mile away, I saw a BP station, across the highway but doable. I chose option 2.

The BP station was newer with a protective covering in the middle over the gas pumps and a large, well-lit, well-provisioned store attached. I propped my bike against the wall and walked in. A smile from behind the counter greeted me, as usual, and I looked around, taking in the warmth.

"Hi, I got a flat. Is it okay if I fix the tire by the propane tanks?" I asked, more out of courtesy than asking for permission.

"Of course!" was her reply.

For some reason, it is almost always the back tire that goes flat, which is more problematic, especially in my case. On the back, I had a pannier rack attached, carrying two eight-pound panniers each, a folded-up tarp for "just in case" reasons, a bike lock that I had not used once on this trip, and a few other miscellaneous items attached one way or another. All of this, plus water bottles, and bike tools, tubes, and levers had to come off before I was able to flip the bike and take off the back wheel.

Everything was greasy and filthy from the day's ride, but I got to work. I have changed many tires in my riding life. Ninety percent of the time, it's the back tire. I have gotten pretty good at it. Wheel off, I quickly found the culprit, a piece of glass the size of a tiny pebble. I ran my fingers several times around the inside tire to make sure nothing else was there that could destroy another tube and proceeded to install the new tube and get merrily on my way.

I have learned you want to throw a little air into the new tube before snapping the tire back on its rim just to be safe. Grabbing my trusty CO_2 air cylinder, I attempted to inflate, but nothing happened. I tried it again. Nothing. Looking closer, I noticed there was something missing on the head. I used this cylinder a few weeks earlier with no problem. I flash back to my last flat outside Ludington and remembered I never did the tire change, the bike shop did.

I was on to the backup, my second option, the hand pump inflator! I have learned to always have a backup for everything bike-related, but especially for moments like this until, of course, option two did not work either. The seal seemed toast, which is possible given this pump hangs on the outside of the down tube on the lower frame and had weathered hundreds of miles on this trip as well as hundreds from all the training rides. Miles, time and weather eventually add up.

Standing there, rain pouring feet away as I hunkered under cover, I got this one second of panic. "Today is Sunday. O-M-G. Even if there is a bike shop in Escanaba, it is closed!"

I stood there, mouth open, panic in my eyes, feeling lonelier than the climber on Everest left behind by his team. I walked inside. I tested Smiley behind the counter about her knowledge of bikes, people with bikes, possible bike shops nearby, anything. Not a point of interest in her life, she said, "I think there was a bike shop at some point in Escanaba." Thanks.

I walked back outside. It was then the pickup drove up, parking in front of the store, feet from my carnage. The pickup was on the downward slope, so to speak, rusty, dented and an oil change away from that big pickup scrapyard in the sky, but to me it offered hope. Mary popped out, looked at me and my sad and panicked eyes and said, "You, okay?" Mary had that striking resemblance to that older woman in the movie "Twister," Meg, who was buried in her house when she was hit by, of course, a twister, and then saved by Bill Paxton and Helen Hunt.

"You don't happen to have a bike pump back there in your little pickup, by any chance?" I replied.

We were off and running. Mary proceeded to mentally and verbally run through her entire personal rolodex of friends and acquaintances who might have some connection to cycling. "Robert was out of town. Glenda's brother I think rides. Ken used to ride until he broke his hip."

Mary continued uninterrupted. Going through her entire list of lifelong associates, randomly Mary then told me about the community park, a half-mile away. "I think there is a bike pump thing-a-ma-jiggy in the park with tools hanging and other stuff but I'm not a biker."

"Seriously?"

"Hop in and I will take you there."

With the assurance from Mary that my bike and stuff were safe, not something I would have even contemplated if back in the urban jungle, I jumped into her pickup, and we were on our way.

Mary was spot on. In the middle of the park, next to the community bike path, was a large, fixed pump with multiple valves and tools hanging off its side. Investigating closer, I knew this would work.

Tire change. It's always the back tire.

On the truck-ride back, thinking to myself about the multi-stepped process of getting everything back together in order and then walking the half mile to the pump, Mary offered, "Throw everything in the back of the truck, and I will take you there." My guardian angel at work.

"Mary, you are a saint."

Back at the park, my bike and sundry bags, bike wheel, and tubes in a pile, I waved Mary off with a big "Thank you," quickly changed the tire, repacked, and was on my way.

The rain was down to a mist, but I didn't care. I had air in both tires! Thank you, Mary! I might get to that Bears game, and their anticipated perfect season, after all.

The ride into Escanaba was joyful. I needed a place to stay, and a bar to watch football, but that would be the easy part after the previous hour or so.

My first stop was the Super 8 but they had no rooms on the ground floor as they were expecting a busload of seniors who booked every room. I could not even fathom why a busload of seniors could be heading up this way, but that was not my immediate concern. They offered a second-floor room, but no elevator nixed that.

Then I stopped at the Sunset Motel, which had okay reviews but became apparent that those reviews originated from close family members looking for a free meal. The sun had clearly set on the Sunset Motel. For me to turn any motel down at this point in the long day is all you need to know to best visualize the appearance of this gem.

My last option was the Hiawatha Motel. Close to the bars with food, working shower, bike allowed in the room. Check, check, check. Plus, I liked the name. Hiawatha, it was! Checking in, I was greeted with an unlocked office door and a smile, both usually good signs. Plus, Clarisa, the office person had a pet seagull, whose name escapes me but clearly had a bad wing and was hanging out for freebies. Kind of reminded me of some of my golf buddies, but I digress.

Clarisa explained that the unnamed seagull loved spaghetti but hated baloney. When I commented that it must be an Italian seagull, she thought that was so funny. It is always nice when people understand good humor.

Motels are an interesting part of our lives. They are like mushrooms that pop up wherever they feel like with little reason as to why. Just like mushrooms, where most people do not know which ones are edible and which ones can kill you, motels are similar as you never really know what you have until you pull out that key and open that door to the room.

Mr. Broken Wing

The first motel, or motor hotel, in the United States is attributed to the Milestone MoTel of San Luis Obispo, California, back in the mid-1920s. As automobiles became more affordable and reliable, people needed places to stay on the lonely two-lane highways spreading out across America. Most, to this day, are individually owned. There is also a resurgence, of sorts, as private equity firms are starting to buy up these run-down days-gone-by's, and refurbish them into trendy, stylish yet affordable places to stay. I could probably recommend 10 or 12 of these run-down gems myself in need of a private equity upgrade given my travels over the prior week or so.

The difference between hotels and motels is the lack of amenities such as free breakfast and the ability to drive right up to your room. This became popular as Mom and Dad, and the 10 kids, unloaded their life's possessions from their paneled station wagons and didn't want to walk that far to do so.

I would guess the next step in this travel housing evolution might be the invention of Cyc-tels, designed specifically for cyclists. Rooms could come equipped with drying devices for shoes and other wet items. Also, an area to clean your bike, maybe with a community hose, bike pumps, and a full array of bike tools would be nice. I personally would add a coffee bar, and beer tappers of local brew, as a special treat to cyclists, but this might be stretching things. Nonetheless, like mushrooms, my goal was always to find that motel that would not kill me.

The room was fine, a word which has a wide range of allowances. My shower had hot and cold, the bed was made and appeared okay, a working post–"Lawrence Welk Show" TV, plus room for the bike. It was fine.

There is something interesting about motels. They all have signs, outside or inside, the room. Usually hand-printed signs, explaining this or that to the first-time patron. This time, the Hiawatha version mentioned nothing about cannabis or air conditioners, just that the TV only worked by hitting the light switch by the door. I could remember that.

Hoping to hit the game at the start, I needed to get all my wet stuff off and rally. With no hair dryers in the room, I noticed one of those rounded heater knobs in the small bathroom which I cranked to eighty and proceeded to spread out everything from cycling shoes, pants, tops, helmet, everything, and closed the door. My makeshift oversized dryer. With a quick shower completed, and clothes on "dry," I was off to see the future world champion Bears.

Mo's Bar was just down the street and had all that I wanted, with a loaded menu of carbohydrate heaven and an impressive array of beer. Entering, I was surprised by a couple of things. One, the pub was full but not too full, and two, there were several Chicago Bear fans in attendance. I figured there would be Cheeseheads wall to wall. For those not from the Midwest, or not fluent in football as a second language, Cheeseheads are the affectionate name for Green Bay Packers fans.

I was able to get a good table up front with my choice of multiple large-screen TVs, and place my cheese curds and beer order, amid banter back and forth with my fellow Bears fans at the tables to my left. Hope is eternal they say, unless you are a Chicago sports fan, where we have kicked hope aside years ago. But we were eager to engage the offseason hype. Justin Fields was supposedly better and Aaron Rodgers, our nemesis, was off to find Broadway fame. At least that was the story we were told.

It didn't take long for the eternity of bad play to overtake the seconds of hope. The game was unfortunately over before it started. The Cheeseheads were in a frenzy as the Bears were down 24-6 early in the third quarter, as I said my goodbyes to my Chicago friends next to me and headed for the exit. After all, I could still watch the game from my room, if a miracle rally somehow surfaced.

Back in my room, I hit the light switch by the door, as instructed, to turn on the TV. Remembering the words from Clarisa that "we get all the stations," I proceeded to attempt to decipher Roku which, apparently, was the moat around any ability to watch TV that night. I didn't have the Roku password. Not again. I called but no answer at the office. Maybe Clarisa was taking the bad-winged seagull for a walk. It became apparent that for the second night in a row, no football for my viewing pleasure was going to happen. Oh, well. There was always tomorrow!

Checking on my makeshift clothes dryer, I was fairly satisfied my shoes and clothes were getting there, maybe half dry.

My thoughts turned to the next day. More rain was anticipated, and I had another issue. I needed to fix or replace my bike pumps. Heading out without those in grade-A shape would tempt the universe to be unkind at the worse possible moment. That I could not risk. Scrolling the internet, I found out there was in fact a bike shop in town, thank God, a Mr. Bike & Ski, but it didn't open until 10 a.m. I hated starting so late, but I had no choice, so I accepted reality, reveled in the thought I could sleep in an hour or two later, and maybe grab a free cup of coffee in the office with Clarisa and Mr. Broken Wing.

Mr. Bike

DAY 11

Sasquatch and the Ten Pointer

When organizing the list of items coming with me on the trip, I did what I had done on previous ones and grabbed flip flops as my sole footwear for all things walking when sans cycling shoes. Weight is weight, and the less the better, but the added dimension of lots of rain made these invaluable, despite the occasional temps in the 40s. Walking across the flooded parking lot to get coffee, my flip flops did the job. Plus, they offered the added benefit that, during drier times, they could be easily attached to the outside of the panniers and put on and off my feet easily.

Waiting on Mr. Bike, I hung out, drank coffee and chatted with Clarisa. She and her boyfriend were from Rockford, Illinois, and loved the country up here and bought the Hiawatha a few years back. She said it has been tough with the Pandemic and all, but they were making it. Mr. Broken Wing seemed uninterested, focused solely on the next free Italian handout. It was time to move on.

Standing by the front door of Mr. Bike at 9:55, day 11 of my journey well underway, my new best friend Jamie saw me standing in the cold mist and hurried to open the door, apologizing. It is hard to imagine any shop owner in Chicago apologizing for anything, let alone for not opening the door prior to the time announced on the painted letters in front. I wasn't sure how to react. I immediately recapped my story, my trip around the lake, the rain, the flat, the oh-for-two pumps.

He immediately went to work on my CO_2 pump while pointing me to the tool section of the store for new hand pumps. Five minutes into my visit, having found the hand pump I wanted, he said, referring to the CO_2 pump, "I think I can fix this," which he proceeded to do. Walking toward the checkout, Jamie pointed to my cycling jersey, inquiring as to its meaning.

I went into the full story, who Danny was and his relevance to the Danny Did Epilepsy Foundation, the impact to my family and the mission of the charity and the people being helped, my ride around the lake so far, as Jamie peppered me with questions. I knew time was getting away and I had another full day, plus dealing with the delayed start, so I finally asked Jamie what I owed him for the service and the new bike pump, and he did his best Mr. Gower imitation from "It's a Wonderful Life" and said, "No charge."

"Huh, what?"

"No charge. We support good causes as part of our biking mission, and I love what you are doing."

Jamie got me out of the rain, fixed my bike pump, and gave me another for free. I was speechless. I just experienced guardian angel number two, within 18 hours. The goodness of humanity struck again.

I think about these bike shop owners and the eventuality of their businesses. Most of the men and women, especially those I've met on this trip, are just good people. They love cycling. They love people who cycle. Yet their enterprise model is so vulnerable to the Internet and are losing business to cheaper prices sourced elsewhere. All the shops could close, and we would still have cheaper prices, but we would lose something, possibly a lot.

That guy, unlocking the door early, to help a distressed cyclist whose pump had broken, is just one example. That local knowledge regarding a simple route adjustment is another. My strong affinity for shops of this sort is even stronger given the past few days. I will buy two bike tubes, instead of one, and always from retail, I pledge, forever, going forward.

Heading west, leaving Escanaba behind me, I had a new quickness to my step. I decided I would be nice to "Karen" from Garmin as she zigged and zagged me out of town, toward my ultimate destination, Menominee. I had been warned by my new best friend, Jamie, this morning that the direct route along Lake Michigan southwest to Menominee was not bike friendly.

I had experienced some unfriendly stretches a few times along this excursion, but this sounded bad. No shoulder, fast and very large trucks. Bad combination for a cyclist. Supposedly, this will change soon as a new surface and wide shoulders are planned for the not-too-distant future, but right now, sorry.

So, I listened to Jamie, and Karen, and followed the voice in my ears instead of the voice in my head. The west and then south route versus direct southwest added 15 to 20 miles, but I knew it was for the best. The roads were nice, and less traveled, and as I slowly shifted from westerly to southwest to south, I finally had some wind at my back. It had not been at my back since the other side of Lake Michigan, somewhere between Ludington and Frankfort in central Michigan, and was much appreciated. It is truly crazy how five miles per hour pushing you from behind versus hitting you in your face changes everything from leg fatigue to spirit.

Plus, the music playing on my earbuds sounded better. Instead of that annoying hum, amidst the whoosh of the wind, you hear crisp music sound. The rain was pretty much gone, annoying other people further east, but not totally. There was one moment where I stopped for lunch, and called Jeanine, who considerately asked about the day and the rain, at which time I looked out in amazement as one large, dark cloud was crushing my bike with rain. Perfect timing once again. I could only laugh. Jeanine had broken the laws of cycling by mentioning the "R" word. Works every time.

One surprise of the day was I got another flat, this time on the front tire. I cannot remember the last time that happened to the front tire. The roads still carried all that grit and dirt from rain before, so changing was a mess, but at least it was quick. I never figured out the cause of this flat, spending more time than usual trying to figure out the why, to no avail.

For the third time on the trip, someone in a pickup truck offered to help. Sensing my dismay as I walked my bike to find someplace I could lean the frame against, he rolled down his window to inquire if I needed a lift or help. I thanked him kindly but gave him the universal wave that all was good. I must admit that sometimes one percent of you feels inclined to accept such a kind offer, especially then, because the rain started up again, but you ultimately say no.

Throughout my trip I continually found good people looking to help. I thought back to years before, my younger years, when I would not hesitate during college to hitchhike, one time the entire way across the state of Wisconsin, or grab a ride from a stranger. Those days are sadly gone, never, I am certain, to return. One of the reasons I launched on this mission initially was that I was tired of the negative news the mainstream media was blasting in my ears, the COVID calamities, political infighting and the rest. I am not someone who has to be transformed into thinking people are, by their nature, good. I knew they were. I just wanted to meet some of them.

Grabbing the new bike pump for the first time, saying another quick "thank you" in my head to Jamie for Mr. Bike being open, and his kindness, I pumped away on the new tube, and was soon rolling again.

At about Powers, Michigan, 30 miles from Escanaba, the route shifted from westerly to due south, and amazingly started a slight but consistent descent all the way into Menominee, at least 45 miles. Wind at my back and a long descent. This is why you are kind to the biking gods—for good moments like this.

Cruising along, you see things that catch your eye. At one point, I was passing a farm with a small pond close to the road. The pond had ducks everywhere. Next to the pond, was a bright red duck house. The house included a single wooden ramp from the water to the coop, a single door and two signs on either side for "Male" and "Female." It took a few feet down the road to figure out the meaning, at which I smiled, appreciating the farmer's humor. You don't want hanky-panky in the duck house.

Another strange sighting was a collection of large and hilarious statues which ranged from a 15-foot Sasquatch to Elsie the Cow in a dress, to a large hot dog man and an oversized T-Rex skeleton with

Sasquatch sighting

party beads. The collection lacked any semblance of synergy but was still worth a photo for proof later. Stumbling across these gems, randomly, makes bike exploration so fun.

It was at this moment, visions of Sasquatch and T-Rex still dancing in my head, when suddenly right in front of me, directly in front of me, straddling the shoulder and the wildflower haven just to the right, was a massive buck deer, with 10 points, maybe more, uncertain what its next move was. I was moving pretty good, probably 18 or 19 miles per hour and approaching quickly. This magnificent collection of horns and fur was just standing there, snorting. As I approached, it didn't just bolt into the woods as I expected. Instead, it started running straight ahead, just to my right, its eyes bulging out and dancing back and forth between me and the road ahead.

I grabbed my brakes but eased my fingers off. How often do you have the opportunity to run with a creature such as this? It was like cycling next to Secretariat. Except this bad boy wanted to go left, across the road, and I was in between his goal and my goal. Common sense told me, "What are you thinking?" but at that moment my instinct told me to keep riding and keep pace. That buck could have lowered its head, stuck its antlers into my spokes and I would have been calling Jeanine from some inadequately staffed urgent care unit in nowhere Michigan. But at that snapshot in time, it was amazing. He continued to run to my right, looking to its left. We both had to be doing 20.

It seemed like an hour but was probably 15 or 20 seconds. Cars were now slowing down to watch. Finally, my male friend had enough and bolted to his right, into the woods. I slowed, catching my breath. No pictures. No TikTok. No witnesses. Just memories.

It didn't escape me that I was on my third leg of the three-leg stool of this ride. The first was Chicago through Gary and up the Michigan western shore. The second leg was St. Ignace west across the Upper Peninsula. The third, south into Menominee, down the eastern shore of Wisconsin, through Milwaukee, into Illinois, and back to Chicago.

The first leg was beautiful with the bounty of great bike paths, less traveled roads, harbor towns, natural forests and varied terrain.

The second was fascinating also for its beauty, but it offered more extremes to experience. I looked with anticipation toward the third. There would be the big-small town of Green Bay, more harbor towns like Sheboygan and urban riding through Milwaukee, followed by northern Illinois and eventually back home to Chicago. Menominee was the next stop as I descended into town.

I had decided to reward myself with a breakfast-included, hot tub-offering institution of relaxation and had found it at the AmericInn. Situated right on the shores of Lake Michigan, I was finally within spitting distance of Central Daylight Time, after a week plus in the Eastern Time Zone. Time was less relevant on this ride. More relevant was whether it was dark outside, light outside or starting to get dark outside again? Much simpler. Thoughts of what laid ahead dancing in my head.

Menominee shore

DAY 12

St. Brendan's Surprise

Entering the third leg heading south to Chicago, 12 days into my ride, I reflected back to the start of this endeavor. I repeatedly got that one question, "Why?" My instinctive response was, "Why not?" Yet it is a bit more than that. So much must come together for this to work, be enjoyable and be successful. You need to be physically in shape. Otherwise, this could be a nightmare. You need to be an experienced cyclist. I am not suggesting you must ride thousands of miles in advance of something like this, but you need to have ridden for enough time, hopefully without large gaps, and enough mileage per ride, to know what you can do.

This experience is essential as you come across surprises along the way, as you most definitely will. Surprises such as flats and other mechanical issues, crazy weather, roads that are not as advertised, and physical issues to your body as you learn what you can, and cannot, tolerate. The last point is so important because you must know when you can power through, and when rest is in order. You learn that a five- or 10-minute break to hydrate, snack or just rest your legs saves you in the long run.

In my case, I started seriously cycling at the age of 30, to train for some cross-country ski racing, but my real push was after seeing a picture or two of myself that I considered less than flattering. It was more than that. I was shocked at how quickly I had gotten out of shape, post-college. At 30, I had just completed my MBA and recently had the second of my three children, plus a full-time job, so there was stuff going on. But seeing that picture was all the motivation I needed. I am now well over twice that age, and I have put on hundreds and thousands of miles every year since.

That brings me to my next point. You must enjoy riding. I have had the fortune to ride on some of the prettiest roads and bike paths in the country, some of which include my regular cycling routes along the Chicago lakefront, and other Chicago area paths. I have done numerous multi-day rides, with large, supported groups, and solo, unsupported, in all corners of the United States, from the great Northwest, through the Midwest, and across New England. Having variety and goals makes training easier.

You also need to have a positive attitude. As I mentioned, things will come up that test your will and determination. The "Why me?" attitude will not get you out of bed on that cold and rainy morning. Also, a positive look on life enables you to see things that others might miss or reject. You suddenly see that 15-foot Sasquatch or T-Rex statue in the middle of nowhere, or that pristine pond along that vintage wooden bridge that stays with you forever.

"Why solo?" I get asked. I love riding with people. I love riding alone. Riding alone, you meet people you might not have met given the dynamics of a group. Going solo, you are forced to engage. Plus, you are totally independent, not having to worry about other cycling members. This might sound selfish, but it creates a different experience.

I have had some people ask me, "Don't you think this is a little crazy at your age?" All I can offer is that it depends on what seat you are looking at the world from. My seat just happens to be a bicycle seat. I understand everyone is different. My bones are getting up there on a relative scale, but my spirit remains young. There will always be aches and pains, but I can only live my life. Cycling makes me younger. As long as my spirit is young, cycling will be part of my life.

So, stay or get in shape; no substitute for putting miles underneath you over a few years. A passion for cycling and a positive look on life are all essential for a trip like this.

I would add one more thing: curiosity. I have been able to ride most of my adult life, and loved it, so those boxes are checked. I view myself as a positive guy also. What drove me on this ride was my curiosity. I knew there would be crazy sightings, interesting people and amazing views potentially around each corner. I was curious to find out what they were.

Northern Michigan and the Upper Peninsula were a mystery to me, and I wanted to experience as much of this as I could, at 17 miles-per-hour.

Lastly, I am very fortunate that I have the time and family support that enables me to pursue this passion. Support is so key. Rides like these are hard enough without dragging that negative energy behind you as you ride.

Sitting at my huge breakfast spread in Menominee, courtesy of the AmericInn, I reflected on the trip so far, and what was still to come. The choices before me included scrambled eggs, pancakes, bacon, Fruit Loops, blueberries, yogurt, water and hot coffee, more than I eat for the whole day normally. "If it's free, it's for me," is my mantra, knowing these calories will be burned off, and necessary.

Plus, I think about those days when even coffee was scarce, and the food was past its expiration date, and I grabbed another piece of bacon, just because. I'm guessing the day-long spinning through western Michigan, the UP, and into Wisconsin has taken off five pounds, probably more. It's not the weight, as much as the feel. You just feel better even with that extra piece of bacon.

The sun, trying to do its part to add to the happy mood, peeks over the eastern horizon of Wisconsin off Lake Michigan, in reds, purples and oranges, right on cue. It was day 12, and I felt it would be a good day as I headed into Green Bay.

Menominee, a town of 8,500, is really one large town split down the middle by the Menominee River with larger Marinette to its south, Menominee to the north. It is the last city in Michigan along this Upper Peninsula route before a quick ride across the river brings you into Wisconsin and the Central Time Zone.

This area, like most I have traveled so far on my ride, was dominated by the Algonquin peoples, and in this case, specifically the

Menominee tribe, but it goes all the way back to the Hopewell peoples several hundred years B.C. and A.D., before vanishing around 600 A.D. At one point in the mid-1800s, it produced more lumber than any other city in the United States.

I was expecting 60 mostly flat miles on this day. If there was any wind, it would likely push me from behind. The day was lighter than most, and I looked forward to getting into Green Bay for a variety of reasons. One is that the ride is partially along the lake, which is always inspiring. Another reason is that I was contacted by the local NBC TV station in Green Bay. They wanted to interview me the next morning about my ride. The producer there had heard about my trip and mission through a friend, and they thought the combination of my trip, my age and the fact I was raising money for a good cause might resonate with the good people of Green Bay.

Lastly, a few years back, and the last time I had stepped foot in Green Bay, I had the fortune to sail on a 210-foot Norwegian square-rigger schooner from Chicago to Green Bay. I was with my daughter and good friends, and although I was an experienced sailor, was unsure what to expect.

This sailing vessel was built in 1927 and captured by the German Navy during World War II. It was a German possession until the war's end, ultimately refurbished by the Norwegians and deployed as a training vessel. Being a square rigger, with something like 27 or 28 total sails, it was great for sailing down wind, and horrible for sailing upwind. Our trip was all upwind, into a blistering north wind of 20 to 30 knots, forcing us to zigzag east, and then west, and back again on Lake Michigan, all the time fighting huge 7- to 10-foot waves.

Ultimately, a bunch of the passengers, and half the crew ended up leaving their lunches over the rail, and I was deployed, with my buddy, as well as my daughter, to lend a hand, on lines, sails and anything else the captain barked. The craziest command put us high up into the "yards," the large wooden spars attached to the masts, tethered by a safety line, to wrestle, by hand, the largest sails. We were literally standing on either the wooden spar or an inch-thick wire, tethered in for "safety," pulling sails weighing hundreds of pounds, with crew and like-minded volunteers, as the ship pitched back and forth, and side to side. Slightly crazy.

By the time we finally got to Green Bay, exhausted and well behind schedule, all I could think about was getting my feet on land and a cold beer. Securing the lines, once in Green Bay, as miracles would have it, we found ourselves positioned right in front of Titletown Brewing. The good people of the brewery could not have been more gracious as a shipload of hungry and thirsty sailors descended to their establishment for the next four to five hours.

Years later, I was hoping to see if my memories were fact or fiction, given the general fuzziness recollecting that afternoon in Green Bay.

The trip south from Menominee, once I was across the river and through Marinette, took me along many nice, smaller, comfortable roads with a large chunk along and through the Green Bay West Shore State Wildlife Area, a 9,000-acre nature preserve situated between Menominee and Green Bay. The roads were some of the best yet, the cars were few. It was a quick ride, for the reasons mentioned, and I soon found myself on the outskirts of Green Bay.

You know you are on the outskirts because you keep getting roundabout after roundabout, those crazy traffic circles, heading into town, as well as all the Packers flags on every house. I have discovered most people know how these roundabouts work with other cars and trucks, as they take turns going through, but are clueless when a bicycle enters the mix. A couple of times, I was treated as more of an uninvited guest than just another moving vehicle taking its turn.

I am not sure a proper description of Green Bay would be that of a large-small city or small-large city, but I would probably go with the former. I quickly found myself in old neighborhoods reminiscent of so many older towns in the Midwest, and the homes reminded me of the Mississippi River towns and Great Lake harbor towns of old.

Green Bay goes by many names, Titletown, Bay City, Packerland, Packer City and Cheesehead-ville. Okay, I may have made up that last one, but all the nicknames directed at one certain professional football team is like a knife plunged into the heart of this person who calls himself from the state immediately to the south. With a population of just over 100,000, it is somewhere around 275th in size in the U.S. and only the third largest in its own state, hardly warranting a professional sports franchise. But if pure results matter, then I will put my jealousy to the side for now, accept it and move on.

Founded by one Jean Nicolet, this location was one of the oldest permanent European settlements in America. As long ago as the 1670s, French explorers sailed into Green Bay, up the Fox River and all the way to the Mississippi River looking for access to the Pacific Ocean. Doing most of those travels by canoe makes them even more remarkable.

The Menominee and Winnebago were the predominate Native Americans at the time. Soon after, like most other towns and villages in that era, and this part of the world, the French made way for the British, who gave it back to the Ottawa and then back to the French until finally the American Revolutionary War settled the score and established a whole new direction.

It is on the outskirts of Green Bay that I grabbed lunch and figured out where I wanted to stay for the night. My priorities were the same as always, with a slight adjustment. I wanted to be close to Titletown Brewing Company, downtown, due to my sailing days gone by, as well as NBC's wish to conduct the interview there the next morning. Searching on my phone, one place jumped out at me. Saint Brendan's Inn and Pub!

Wait, what? Are you kidding me?

Located a few blocks from Titletown, right on the Fox River, this Irish inn and pub almost brought tears to my eyes. For those who are not inclined to know, nor be interested, St. Brendan is the patron saint of lost navigators. Saint Brendan had been watching over me this entire trip. He called out to me in that old Irish verse, angels singing, and brought me home to his inn.

The three-story inn has a large stained-glassed dining room, with all the Irish fare, an old vintage bar stolen straight from the Temple Bar of Dublin, and two floors of beautiful hotel rooms. The dining

Irish heaven

room has the feel of a European cathedral, and the bar is that special one where, once they've checked you out, of course, you feel instantly welcome and never want to leave. Who would have thought the most authentic Irish hotel and pub this side of Dublin would be in Green Bay, Wisconsin?

I immediately booked my reservation and headed downtown, straight to St. Brendan's. No second option here, no price shopping, although the price was amazingly cheap. This was my first and only choice. In fact, if there was no room available, I would have just unfurled my tarp, fluffed up my pannier as a pillow and slept in the parking lot.

Riding east into town, the Green Bay downtown strikes you as both a real downtown with real buildings, construction cranes and the full array of urban stuff, yet a lot smaller. It's kind of a cool complement between big and small, and the setting is special with the bay and

Fox River merging. The Inn is even better than I could have hoped. Storing my bike in the copier room, literally leaning it against the copier, the staff were alarmingly welcoming. Discovering we had friends in common from Chicago, we were immediately best friends, creating an air of hospitality so long gone in this post-pandemic era. I instantly felt like I was at a fine downtown hotel in Galway.

The room was the nicest on the trip, by a factor of a lot, or whatever is after a lot. Entering, I saw a grand, king-sized bed with more comforters and pillows than I probably had, collectively, in my life up until the day I left for college, pristine welcoming walk-in shower, mahogany everywhere. And a hair dryer. In my present state of grunginess, I had that feeling I really didn't belong nor deserved such fine amenities and felt that at any moment the fun police would show up and take all of this from me.

But I kept that to myself. I almost didn't want to leave. Nonetheless, the pub bar beckoned, and I had Guinness to drink. I cleaned up quickly, eager to explore.

St. Brendan's pub

I really did not have any master plan, other than taking the elevator from the third floor to the first, so I reached out to a nephew, Jimmy, who lived on the outskirts of Green Bay and invited him to join me for a Guinness, and whatever followed. The problem was he couldn't get there until 6 p.m., and it was only 4 p.m.

What would I do? What does any person of Irish descent do in such a predicament? If not already part of the Patriot team of tee-totalers, he bellies up to the bar and has "the first of the day," of course.

The bar is majestic, emitting an air of "The Quiet Man" and the Ashford Castle with its heavy, carved oak and comfortable swivel chairs. Having passed the eye test with Mike, the bartender, I immediately ordered the first of the day, and then moved to the menu for an appropriate appetizer.

Having not eaten since my AmericInn breakfast hours earlier, I was starving. There was the usual Irish fare such as Dublin Mussels, Curry fries, and Emerald Isle crab cakes. But for some reason, cheese curds jumped out at me. Maybe it was the locale or Wisconsin hypnotism for all things cheese but that is what I ordered. Guinness and cheese curds. What doesn't kill you, makes you stronger. Now this item was listed under Appetizers, so that is what I assumed I would get, a limited portion of pre-food. What arrived was something that could have fed the Army of the Potomac from the Civil War. It was huge, but again, this was Wisconsin. Of course, I jumped right in.

The bar had a couple of the usual local types one would expect. First-name basis, local chatter dominating the conversational flow. I jumped in when appropriate. Finally, the conversation moved to me, why I was there, and why anyone would ride a bike even as far as a city block, let alone around Lake Michigan. We had a few laughs, all at my expense, as I worked through my cheese curds and Guinness, ever mindful that the fun police could be lurking at any moment and scurry away with one of my precious curds, or the last gulps from my stout.

It was a lovely pregame as they call it in Green Bay, as I waited on my nephew. Between the feel of a tighter core from the days of full-day riding, and the expansive natures of Guinness and cheese curds, my stomach was trying to wrestle with what the heck was going on down below. It was blasting out that submarine announcement of "Dive! Dive!" as the enemy was sighted.

My stomach was making strange sounds, not unlike when the Hindenburg attempted, poorly, to dock at the ill-fated mooring mast, and then exploded. That ended badly. So, could this. *"I don't feel good, I need to lie down,"* I was thinking, maybe even a quick nap, when Jimmy walked through the door, and we started all over again.

The dining room was as lovely, and well-apportioned, as the bar. I ordered shepherd's pie for no good reason, knowing there was no way I could even finish off the peas, let alone the whole pie. I knew I would have to hold up my honor, of course, given I was the inviter, and he is my nephew. Dinner arrived. More Guinness.

I was catching up on all things with my nephew, Green Bay and my ride, when I saw a blur out of the corner of my eye, and it was heading straight toward our table. It was my 3-year-old grandson, saying, "Papa! Papa!" much louder than the room required but the best sound I had heard in a couple of weeks. Trailing behind, as not to steal little Johnny's thunder, were my daughter and her husband, up from Chicago, on a mission to surprise.

When you have had limited face-to-face conversations with other humans, and no family one-on-ones whatsoever for a few weeks, punctuated by long stretches of golden silence, this moment comes at you like a firehose. The processing part is delayed.

Little Johnny snapped me back to reality, that special moment, as he climbed up on my lap, looking for food. We were instantly all around the table, ordering drinks, more food, talking about the ride, and me sharing my shepherd's pie with whomever would partake. I was eager to share.

The next day would be another half-day. I had agreed to meet up with the film crew from NBC at Titletown Brewing in the morning, so that would take out a half day. For the first time in days, I didn't have to rush home and hit the hay. I ordered another Guinness, as did my

St. Brendan's gang

support team, and the night continued. The revelry finally ended with our waiter telling us they were closing for the night and we must leave as we were the only patrons remaining. We got the hint.

NBC interview

DAY 13

NBC and Little Nolan Ryan

The next morning started with a headache, but quickly moved in a positive direction with an amazing St. Brendan's breakfast, a repacking of the bike and a quick ride to Titletown. The reporter and production crew suggested a place next to the brewery but outside, close to the Fox River, and in between the river and a large parking lot. My daughter, Erin, son-in-law Joe and little Johnny decided to accompany me to the interview, standing off to the side, just out of view of the camera. The day looked grand as the sun was in full bloom, the skies were blue, and the wind was light.

Setting up for the shoot, Chris, the reporter, went through his litany of anticipated questions, formulating a plan. The questions were as expected, asking about the ride, motivations, hardships.

He started it off with "We have with us John McShea, who is riding his bike solo around Lake Michigan. John, tell us about the ride and why you are doing it?"

Me: "Well, this whole endeavor has been amazing. I started off from Chicago, headed east and then north up the Michigan shore to Mackinaw City, across the Upper Peninsula and now Green Bay. My goal is to finish up in Chicago over the next couple of days. It started as a ride, and I added the charity component which took on a life of its own."

Chris: "This is your 13th day, correct? How many miles did you ride in total?"

Me: "I am hoping to complete it in 15 days. Probably 1,100, maybe 1,150 by the end."

Chris: "What has been the toughest part?"

Me: "Probably the rain. I bet I have had at least seven or eight days of rain. The wind has been in my face most of the way also. The hills in northern Michigan also had their moments. That being said, it hasn't been that bad, really. I have been able to see some really cool places and meet many nice people. Overall, it's been pretty good."

Chris: "Tell me about the charity you rode for."

Me: "I decided to use this ride to raise money for an organization named Danny Did, named after Danny Stanton, a beautiful 4-year-old who passed away in his sleep from an epileptic seizure. Very heartbreaking as you can imagine. The foundation raises money to provide seizure monitors for families facing epilepsy. We have been able to raise $8,000 for this cause."

Chris: "That's pretty cool. I would put you in the more mature age range. How has your body held up?"

Me: "Given the conditions, I would say pretty well. My left Achilles and right lower back talk to me once in a while, but overall, I'm pretty good so far."

Chris: "Give us some insights on some memorable moments."

Me: "I would say my ride through Sleeping Bear Dunes was one I will never forget. Also, I stayed mostly in motels. There have been some crazy ones on my trip."

Chris: "Any flats or bike breakdowns?"

Me: "Yeah. I have had three flats, two on my back tire and one on my front. Nothing else bike-related, thank God. Hopefully that is all behind me."

Chris: "Any advice for the novice rider thinking of doing something like this?"

Me: "Sure, as Nike says, just do it. There are a lot of cool places to visit and nice people out there. You just have to find them."

With that, the interview was coming to a conclusion.

Their plan was to put this in the "uplifting" category of their news hour as they focused on the long ride, the charity behind the ride, the money raised, my age and the overall feel-good story. I was happy to oblige.

As we were getting close to wrapping up, I heard a loud sound, not unlike a rock hitting a windshield. I then noticed a blur out of the corner of my eye, as Johnny was being picked up in a flash and whisked away out of view. Pretending not to notice the commotion, I finished the interview, later to learn, the sound, most definitely, was a rock thrown by the little one and hitting some innocent office worker's windshield. Thankfully, no damage resulted, but a couple of said child's parents were mortified. Thankfully it was the little one's changeup, and not his fastball.

Interview completed, I thanked Chris and his crew for the opportunity and said adios to my family threesome. I was motivated to get on the road. The route would be close to 80 miles taking me through and out of Green Bay and into Manitowoc, and ultimately to Sheboygan, the land of brats.

The first leg was beautiful as I left downtown and hooked onto the Fox River Trail bike path for at least 15 miles, curving this way and that along the river, and then turning, first westerly and then south. My destination would take me southeast as I traveled across the Door Peninsula, and Kewaunee County, first on a long, narrow, but well-shouldered county road named Mill Road and then on to the Devil River State Trail for 13 or 14 miles.

In a small oddity, while riding along Mill Road, I was passing a golf course, and evidently, its driving range, when I noticed to my surprise a driving range ball hopping down the road, just to the left of my moving bike, and still rolling. Stopping right on my path, I slowed and then picked up the gift, ever wondering who the mighty young golfer could have been that tagged that drive so much farther than any of the other range balls left to die on the cut grass, yards and yards back.

Once on the Devil River State Trail, I immediately saw that the surface was that dreaded crushed limestone. To my surprise and delight, this time it was super flat, rock hard, and extremely well

Devils River State Trail

maintained. It was also incredibly straight with intermittent bridges and tall, sloping forest on both sides, running along parts of Devil River, with little in the way of intersecting roads. You could see well past a mile down the road. It was delightful. The wind was still on my back, so the combination of great paths and roads took me to the outskirts of Manitowoc in the early afternoon, quicker than I imagined.

Manitowoc is like several of the towns and cities recently visited, where parts of the town look to be on life support while other areas exhibit a resurgence of hope in the form of new restaurants, businesses and housing. As an endpoint to the S.S. Badger, as the ferry travels back and forth from Ludington, Michigan, the harbor dominates all things Manitowoc. At its height, there were 14 such vessels that frequented this route. Now there's only one. You sense that once the last ferry on this part of the lake shuts down for good, which is the rumor, much of this harbor will also.

The history of the town is rinse-and-repeat to that of other lakefront towns along the Great Lakes. Native American peoples controlled it for centuries, Europeans showed up, Americans moved progressively west from the east coast, across the Appalachians, into the Midwest and beyond, taking land as they came, Native Americans moved even further west, and eventually, Native Americans were resettled. Manitowoc in the Menominee language means "place of the spirits," which kind of tells you what they thought of this region.

Nonetheless, there was no stopping progress. In this case though, there was a treaty established declaring the transfer of title in 1836, the Treaty of the Cedars, from the Oneida and Brothertown peoples to the United States. This was a transfer of 4,000,000 acres for the rich sum of $700,000, or 17 cents per acre. I would guess $700,000 went a lot further in those days.

Also, interestingly, the year before, in 1835, President Andrew Jackson authorized land sales for the region to various speculators, possibly accelerating the need for the Treaty. I meant to check whether there were any of President Jackson's close relatives coincidently living in the area at the time those land transfer decisions were made.

Two bizarre and somewhat disturbing facts popped up when looking at Manitowoc's past. The first is that they were on the receiving end, in 1962, of a piece of the Russian satellite Sputnik 4 that broke off and somehow re-entered the atmosphere and crashed on North 8th Street. This, as you can imagine, made quite a stir.

Alarmed by the bad press, the Russians wanted their piece of metal back, but this was not granted before a cast was made by some industrious locals to highlight the important event. As proof that there is an entrepreneur everywhere, this copied piece of metal now resides in the Rahr-West Art Museum, in full display, as an icon to state-funded, poorly engineered Russian technology.

Secondly, and sadly, Manitowoc was historically a sundown town, well into the 1960s, forcing non-whites to leave town before sundown. There is not much more to say there, except that the townspeople finally saw the evil of their ways and put this behind them.

Sheboygan was just another 26 miles down the road. I had visited Sheboygan a few years back by sailboat, and I was really impressed with what they had done with the harbor and lakefront around the Sheboygan River. The downtown was fun with a fresh vibe.

With the wind still favorable, I had under an hour and a half in my head. You automatically take wind at your back for granted until those flashbacks appear, those remembrances of only a few days earlier when the wind would literally grab your handlebars and not let go. Halfway to Sheboygan, the weather gods awoke from their slumber. They wanted my handlebars.

The wind shifted from north to east and then southeast, the temperature strangely dropped 10 degrees and the cold rain began. First it came in rolling waves off Lake Michigan on my port side and then a blinding deluge. All I could do was laugh. One moment I was in cycling nirvana and the next minute I was, once again, in the full cycle bike wash. It was a stinging type of sleet. "Where-the-F did that come from?" was all I could manufacture. My average rolling mile-per-hour instantly dropped from 18 to 12.

I realized it was going to take me longer than an hour and a half.

Due to some unexpected route alterations, my "half day" ride from Green Bay was staring at a mid-80-handle in terms of mileage, with the weather gods fighting me tooth and nail. I plunged ahead. The route took me along Lake Michigan the whole way, first on Lakeshore Drive and then Lakeshore Road. You would think the Sheboygan Department of Creativity would intervene and suggest some other name just to spice things up. How about Stinging WTF Rain Pellets Road? Probably won't happen.

Just before Sheboygan, I pulled to the side to take in the huge stone sign announcing I was at the entrance to Whistling Straits, the famous golf mecca, and host of three PGA Championships and one Ryder Cup. This has been the site of incredible drama and multitudes of lost golf balls never to be seen again, whether it is due to the tall dune grass, ponds, innumerable sand dunes or, lastly, Lake Michigan, itself. I can speak from personal experience of all the above. I pushed on.

Sheboygan goes by either the Bratwurst Capital of the World, or the City of Cheese, Chairs, Children and Churches, which is way too long. You wonder how many city council members it took to think up that one. I will go with the brats. In fact, I did.

Finding a Johnsonville brat was my mission, which in Sheboygan is not hard. It's like finding a Smith in Salt Lake City, or an incarcerated politician in Illinois. One does not have to look very far. My options for food were many and I picked the Black Pig, located downtown and out of the rain. With a full array of local beer and a menu that had everything pig related, I settled in, one eye on the dark clouds outside, the other on my humongous brat I was about to devour.

It started to pound rain outside. I kept eating. Eventually the rain slackened off and I knew I had to find a place to rest my head. My mission as usual was to find someplace interesting and affordable to reside for the night. My two options were the Harbor Winds Motel or the Rest Inn. I know you should never decide based solely on the motel's name, but I did. My previous experience with a motel with the name Harbor in it was not altogether special. Given the last hour, adding wind in the name was an immediate pass. It looked like it would be the Rest Inn. Sounded good. How bad could it be? I was soon to find out.

Walking in, there was no one behind the front desk.

"I'm sure they will be right back," I thought.

Nope. I called the lobby phone in the hope that it might be forwarded. Nope. Finally, a young lady—I will call her Ms.

Indifference—appeared and offered that empty apology heard a few times on this trip, citing the lack of staff today. And then she told me she was on her break.

Wait, what?

That was the first sign I should have bolted and headed to the Harbor Winds. But, of course, I didn't. I'm tough. I had ridden those hills by Sleeping Bear, for God's sake. It takes more than a simple inconvenience to set me back. I checked in, rolled my bike down the hall, opened my door and was immediately hit with the smell of dog poop, which obviously had been dropped on the room carpet by a recent tenant, right by the door as you walked in. Looking up I saw the sight of an unmade bed and towels on the floor. I made the decision immediately I didn't need to check out the bathroom.

Marching back to the front desk, Ms. Indifference offered that same weak apology I had just heard minutes ago, offering up again the lack of staff that day, and booked me into another room. It was evident she had no idea what was going on in the Rest Inn, nor did she remotely care.

Opening door number two, I had already made up my mind there would not be door number three. Relieved that no animal waste smell immediately filled my nostrils and the bed apparently made, I walked in to give it further review. It was, well, okay. The shower had mold on the ceiling, the TV remote was missing a back cover and the chair had cigarette burn marks all over the arms of the chair, but I was tired. I had had a long day, and another was in store the next day as I was hoping to make it to Kenosha. I just did not want to start this process all over again at some other place.

I was slightly unnerved at that point and didn't care to unleash the covers, so I grabbed the large blanket jammed in the closet, and spread it out over the bed and pillow, in hopes of some semblance of rest at the Rest Inn.

That was when the dog began to bark.

It was not that deep guttural bark you hear from a big dog, but more that high-pitched *yip* from those tiny dogs often confused with a cat. I couldn't figure out where it was coming from, but I knew it was close. Maybe it was the offender from room number one. It kept barking. I called the front desk as a joke, knowing there would be no answer. Nope. With no other option, I grabbed some of the extra blankets and covered my head, cursing Mini-Cujo, the evil one.

DAY 14

West Nile or Zika?

The morning came too soon. Not wanting to stay at the Rest Inn any longer than necessary, I quickly got organized, hoping to grab the advertised breakfast on the way out. Heading to the breakfast room, I could not help but notice there was no one behind the front desk. I was sure she was on a much-needed break and would be right back.

Walking into the lobby area designated for serving breakfast, it became immediately apparent the breakfast was not as advertised. Either the Kenosha Kickers polka band cleaned out the place prior to my 6:30 arrival, or someone failed to stock the place the night before. I will go with the latter.

Nonetheless, going with my life rule of "if it's free, it's for me," I grabbed random items of what was left in an attempt at breakfast. One rather hard English muffin, one pink yogurt and a banana to go. Plus, the coffee was cold. I was thinking I needed to leave quickly before I did something I would later regret. That was when an elderly couple walked in, carrying a rat dressed as a dog. We, meaning the rat-dog and me, instantly locked eyes.

You! I attempt to burn a hole through its skull with my eyes. All I got back was an indifferent tweak of a smile. Why not, this was the land of indifference. My good vibes, built up over two weeks, had vanished. It was time to leave, and quickly. Front desk still unattended, I dropped off my key. I rolled my mount out the front door, most certainly never to return.

Opposite: Sunflowers

Despite the weak breakfast, my 14th day on the road greeted me with a smile. It was hard to believe it had been two weeks already with only two days of riding left. The rain had passed through, now bothering people further north, up in Wisconsin and Minnesota. To complete the theme, the wind was on my nose once again. I counted eight days of rain out of the 13 so far with most days adding unfavorable winds as well. I looked forward to what the weather gods had in store for the last two days. Hail? Snow? Locusts?

I have learned anything is possible cycling in the Midwest. My plan was to make it to Kenosha late in the day, a distance of 103 miles or so, by way of Kohler, Port Washington, Milwaukee and Racine. I knew it was aggressive, but I would love an easier ride on my last day. It would be a different type of ride than I had done up to that point. First, I would be traveling through central Wisconsin on rolling hills nestled right up to the shores of Lake Michigan, then into and through the urbanity of Milwaukee, and then the large harbor town of Racine, and into Kenosha.

The beauty of this route, besides the stretches along the shores of Lake Michigan, were long, paved bike paths interconnecting all the way into Milwaukee. First, you have the Sheboygan Interurban Trail, which starts just south of Sheboygan and takes you nine miles south until you connect on to the Ozaukee Interurban Trail for another 30 glorious miles and a final 10 miles on the Oak Leaf Trail into northern Milwaukee. This was literally bike path heaven.

The Sheboygan Interurban Trail is one of the oldest in the country created by visionaries of old. The land was originally owned by the Milwaukee Electric Railway & Light Company, an electric railway that once ran between Milwaukee and Sheboygan in the early 1900s until 1951. During its operation, it was made famous for transporting African American blues musicians to the main recording studio for Paramount Records' recording label in Port Washington and ultimately, in Grafton, Wisconsin.

The idea of African American blues musicians from the rural South traveling to Wisconsin in the late 1920s and early 1930s to cut recordings by taking the "electric train" seems amazing today, especially given the "sundown" laws still going on just to the north.

Lying dormant after 1951, the stretch was converted into multi-use paths and eventually connected with other paths, north and west.

The Ozaukee Interurban Trail is the core between Sheboygan to the north and Oak Leaf Trails to the south, running for 30 miles along woodlands, farmlands, wetlands and waterways including the Milwaukee River, Lake Michigan and the Lake Michigan National Marine Sanctuary, a newly designated area of 962 square miles located out in the waters of Lake Michigan protecting shipwrecks and other important, and potentially fragile, habitat. The route is stunning, which I uncovered at every turn.

The Oak Plank is the final leg into Milwaukee proper. Total trail distance for Oak Plank is more than 135 miles around Milwaukee County, but for me and my route I only needed 10 or so until urban bike lanes demanded my attention.

Despite the wind, still freshly in my face, I rode on from one trail to the next, occasionally being rudely interrupted by a state highway or county road heading east and west across my path. I was back in the zone, earbuds turned off, the quiet stunning and the ride glorious. The path was relatively flat, winding left and right, as I passed state parks; tall, wooded forests; sand dunes and dune grasses that never get old; and marsh wetlands.

I entered the Belgium Waterfowl Production Area, stopping to read the sign, "Come forth into the light of things, let nature be your teacher," by William Wordsworth. I took this to heart. I didn't know Wordsworth, but his words resonated. I also didn't know I was about to be taught about this nature thing in the most painful of ways.

This area is a major migratory stopover for fowl of all types, and the diversity of terrain along this route is overwhelming. I could not get enough of all things seen and heard when, once again, the cycling gods awoke from their slumber. They just could not let me be. I was rolling along in a stretch of lowlands, along marshland on both sides, sun and south winds now warming the air, when I got that feeling. Again, the back tire. Not possible. I knew I should have never made that comment during my NBC interview.

I shouted the four-letter "F" word about the other four-letter "F" word. This time, I was in the middle of nowhere. This was my fourth flat on the trip, more than I expected. I usually can ride a whole season without one flat. The daily grind was taking its toll.

Thinking back, the first three flats a half mile from Ludington, outside Escanaba, and on the way to Menominee were all in the rain, after long days of riding. This time it was in the warm sunshine.

Looking for relief, all I saw were uninterrupted bike paths as far as I could see, up the path and back behind. To my right and left, just lilly pads, croaking toads and scummy pond water on both sides as far as I could see. The air was still. There was no BP station to save me this time. No pickup truck to hop into. I had to change this tire on my own, and quickly. I really had no other choice. It must get fixed. Quickly, because I had seen this movie before, in a similar setting, and I knew what comes next.

Mosquitoes.

I leaned my Trek Terror against the only possibility nearby, a bike path sign declaring the mile where I was marooned as well as the location where they would find my body once those bloodthirsty mosquitoes discovered I was in the neighborhood. Quickly I went to work. Panniers off, other crap off. Pannier rack loosened and off. I flipped the bike to keep the chain and gears from getting totally immersed in the muck and removed the back tire.

Two bikers came around the corner from behind and yelled out, "Need help?" Cyclists by nature are good people, but they are human. They do not want to stop any more than I wanted to be sitting there playing bike doctor in the swamp. I thanked them and waved them on. After all, I had everything I needed: tubes, tools, pumps.

They looked relieved and rode on. I went back to work. Looking for the cause, I found a tiny, minute piece of wire that must have been stuck in the tire somehow and finally punctured the tube. I could not even see it from the outside of the tire. I just felt it by running my fingers along the inside.

Putting the new tube in, and at my most vulnerable point in the process, the leader of the mosquito army attacked, followed by his angry horde. I needed to inflate the tire as fast as I could and get out of there. I was pumping and swatting, pumping and swatting, pumping and swatting.

Mosquitoes were biting my legs, my arms, inside my ears. It was a swarm of mosquitoes like something out of "The Ten Commandments" or "The Mummy." It certainly felt biblical. I flashed to that Deet mosquito spray I packed but never even thought about using, packed somewhere in the bowels of my two panniers. Forget about it. No time.

Another set of riders passed by. This time I didn't even wait for the proverbial question of kindness, and I said, louder than probably necessary, "I'm fine!" No wasted conversations, motions, nothing. I just wanted to inflate, re-attach and get up to whatever speed is a half-a-mile-per-hour faster than mosquitoes can fly. Tire re-attached, chain grease everywhere, I reconnected the pannier rack, then the panniers and the other crap, wiped my hands on something green and hopefully not poisonous, and headed back on the path, never looking back.

I thought I heard tiny mosquito voices saying, "Hey, come back. Don't leave us. That was fun," but I may have imagined that.

Picking up speed, I was convinced I was certain to wake up in the middle of the night in some Kenosha dive, in a cold sweat, taking my last breaths due to West Nile or Zika virus, or some other mosquito death trap floating through central Wisconsin.

Lunch could not come soon enough. Between the weak Rest Inn breakfast and limited sleep, hard miles and brutal mosquito attack, I was hungry and uncomfortably itchy and needed to stop. I saw a bar and restaurant right off the bike path, and next to the Wisconsin River, and decided to give it a shot. I had 40 or so miles done and wanted to ride through Milwaukee before stopping again.

The Stilt House was the answer. Great food with a full offering of local beer, typical of every place I had wandered into since I hit Wisconsin. I passed on the brew given my long miles still ahead.

As always, I took more time than needed, as I sat outside, enjoying the late morning warmth, the wholesome Midwest fare, all the while scratching my resting legs. With the number 60, as in miles to go, flashing in my head, I finally left my seat of refuge and jumped back on my seat of exploration.

The route took me from the Ozaukee right to the Oak Leaf Trail for the next 10 miles, dumping me right in front of the Milwaukee Art Museum. This area on Milwaukee's far east side is stunning and one of the best-kept secrets in America. It has a huge, manicured lawn around the Art Museum, highlighted by three amazing structural masterpieces by world-renowned architects Calatrava, Kahler and Saarinen.

In full view as I passed were the beautiful Milwaukee Harbor, the Summerfest grounds, the Lakeshore State Park, BMO Pavilion and the American Family Amphitheater. All located together on the intersection of Lake Michigan and the mouth of the Milwaukee River, it's worth a day, or week, just checking it all out, but especially cool by bike. I really wanted to just hang there for the entire day, but I knew I still had 40-plus miles before the day was done.

My route took me along the lakeshore, into the historic Third Ward and across the river on Water Street. This area reminded me of southside parts of Chicago with heavy industry that was a mix of days-gone-by and new enlightenment. The historic Third Ward is one of Milwaukee's oldest neighborhoods, originally populated by Irish emigrants looking for a better life, but now it's Milwaukee's best collection of the arts, fine dining, shopping and lakefront fun. This is where all of Milwaukee's top festivals take place.

The Third Ward has a long history in Milwaukee's story. Two events devastated the people from this ward. The first one was the sinking of the Lady Elgin in 1860 as it left Milwaukee, causing more than 400 people to perish, the second greatest loss of life on the Great Lakes ever.

The second was the Great Third Ward Fire of 1892. The fire started at a paint factory situated on the Milwaukee River and fueled by 50-mph winds, and it quickly spread to many of the ward's buildings, eventually displacing almost 2,000 people, almost all Irish Americans. There was no insurance or backup plan in those days besides the Catholic churches and family, to ease the pain.

Through the Third Ward and safely across the river, the route slowly transitioned through South Milwaukee and its heavy factories and warehouses to emerging suburbia. This is where I reconnected with the Oak Leaf Trail. The next stretch was mostly connecting from one path to the next on such bike connectors as MRK Trail, the Root River Pathway and the County Bike Trail, heading southeast toward the outskirts of Racine.

Milwaukee Art Museum

The Root River Pathway takes you along the river, so named, and the peaceful route was much appreciated as the miles ticked on. I was close to 90 miles in at that point and was hallucinating about my cheeseburger in paradise and a cold draft beer. Wisconsin is really blessed to have so many fantastic opportunities to ride, and ride safely, and the wonder of it all almost made this last leg enjoyable, if not for the previous 90.

Choosing to ride around Racine, I targeted downtown Kenosha 12 miles due south. The route was almost entirely on the County Bike Trail. My $9 ear buds were still blasting like new to vintage Neil Young, Old Crow and the Dead, with my head down and pumping, I continued to celebrate every 10-mile increment with the proverbial "Boom!" In addition, "Karen" from Garmin had found the evils of her ways and was behaving.

The suggested route through central Wisconsin and Milwaukee was invaluable and spot on. It does help when you have interconnected bike paths and the voice in your ear is aware of them.

On one of my post-lunch, leg-stretching, one-last-attempt to scratch that unreachable mosquito bite located right in the middle of my back, I decided to research my last night on this trip. I was praying it did not include strange men from Oz, bed bugs, cigarette burns, barking dogs, airplane-engine-sounding air conditioners, or psycho-themed rooms. I was getting selective in my old age. I came across the Wyndham Kenosha Harborside, and decided this was the place for me.

I knew there was harbor in the name but after the previous night, I got past that. Plus, I had stayed in Wyndhams in the past and usually they understand what running a hotel is all about. While looking, I noticed one other thing. Right across the street, a few feet from my hotel door, was a burger bar by the name of Captain Mike's. Nautical-themed burger bar? Are you kidding? It was meant to be.

Pulling up, a little after five in the late afternoon, 104 miles done with the same number of mosquito bites as miles on the day, I walked in to see, to my amazement, an actual individual behind the front desk, smile plastered on her face, looking to make my day. I looked around. The lobby was active and very clean. Shiny coffee pots offering free still-hot coffee. New large screen TVs were barking out the latest Packers news or local weather. I was immediately unsettled by the positive and clean nature of this establishment. I tried to recall if my lunch included any mushrooms that may have gone hallucinogenic on me. Nope, this was real. Exhaling, I walked up to Ms. Smiley behind the desk.

"Of course, we have a room."

"No problem on the bike in your room, I will get you an extra sheet."

"Of course, we serve a full breakfast, starting at 6:30."

"Captain Mike's has the best burger in town," were her rapid, joyful responses as I hammered her with questions.

Damn it, I deserve this. I said a silent "thank you" to all of the higher spirits for this amazing welcoming.

Taking my time, I took the longest shower of the trip. Full shower accoutrements, nice. No duct tape on the TV remote. Perfect. No handwritten, random signs pointing out the obvious, good. Fresh

Captain Mike's

linens and towels, stop it. "Damn it," I repeat again to no one but maybe out loud, "I deserve this."

Freshly scrubbed, I got organized for the final day. It would be a short day. I hadn't even looked at the route, but I guessed it was 50 miles, all in. I searched deep through my panniers for my last least-smelly, least-worn shorts and shirt, looking to present myself well to Captain Mike. Finding anything remotely wearable at this stage of a long trip is a little challenging. It's like trying to find that lost parking voucher at two in the morning after a night out. Even those wearable items that I had pulled into the shower at some point on the trip to freshen would likely be immediately chucked to the side by your average homeless person.

I did what I could. I grabbed shorts and a Margaritaville-themed short-sleeve T-shirt, both worn several times, including the previous day, and my trusty flip flops. I was ready. Burger Time!

Walking out the automatic hotel doors, I was one step on my way to see Captain Mike when the first large, wet drop hit me, squarely on the forehead.

Seriously?

It didn't look like it would rain an hour ago. Then more. Same size, same wetness. On a mission and not to be denied, I bolted in between the drops and into Captain Mike's.

Vito, my bartender, greeted me with "Ehhh, how ya doing?"

"Great, I'm flipping to my flops, and avoiding the drops!" I responded. He smiled.

I bellied up to the bar. After a quick look, yet already knowing my complete order hours ago, I responded, "Captain Mike Burger and a good bourbon, on the rocks."

We were off to the races. Vito is friendlier than I found further north. He even started a conversation before I did. Changes in latitudes, changes in attitudes, I guess.

"I don't recognize you, what brings you to Kenosha?" he asked.

I proceeded to tell my story one last time about the ride around the lake, why I chose to do it solo, the days of rain and wind, my route. The couple on my left next to me overheard, and jumped in. Between the couple, the bartender, and now the guy in the Brewers hat to my right, I got the usual questions I had heard throughout my trip.

"Why didn't you do it in a group?"

Not what I wanted. Different dynamic.

"Who carried all your stuff?"

I did.

"How much did all your stuff weigh?"

Probably 20 pounds.

"Doesn't your butt hurt?"

No, not really.

"Did you camp?"

No, motels.

"How were the motels?"

They had their moments.

"What did you do when it started raining?"

I kept riding.

"Did you have any flats?"

Yes, four.

"Who fixed them?"

I did.

Each question led to more questions, and a lot of comments. Vito, the couple on my left and Mr. Brewer fan all had friends who were "big riders" but none of them appeared to have been on a bike of any type in decades. The comments were lighthearted, and usually at my expense, questioning the "why?" I talked about the charity behind the ride, the cause, the money raised. They all knew someone affected by epilepsy and congratulated me on the effort. The couple to my left handed me a $20 bill, asking if I would put it toward the cause.

"Of course. You are very kind."

Remember, Bears fans, there are good people everywhere, even Wisconsin. I bought a round of drinks for the group. I talked in detail about the hills and rain of Sleeping Bear, the ride across the UP and discovering the Bates Motel, the Hiawatha and the pet seagull, and St. Brendan's. The Brewers fan told me, "I have to start riding again," with the others nodding in agreement. I have heard that a lot on this trip. I hope they do.

Way past my bedtime at this point, I finally bid my adieu, noticing the bill looked considerably lighter than it should have. I guess Vito enjoyed my stories. Running between drops, I was back at the Harborside, and thinking of day 15.

Ready to beat the rain

DAY 15

Home

Waking to that now familiar popcorn sound, I checked the weather. Ugh. It looked nasty. It looked like it would rain all day. It wasn't that weather map highlighted by just green either. It was that multi-colored dark green, yellow and red that told me we were going to have some fun. Why would this day be any different?

My plan for the last day was to rendezvous at the house of my daughter (of St. Brendan's fame), for a celebratory bar-b -que. She lives on the northwest side of Chicago and is close to great bike paths that travel north and south into the city.

Easy, peasy.

For the first time on this trip, I had an urgency not inflicted by me, for me. I hate to think I am late and am keeping others waiting. It is a curse I have carried with me since being a kid. It is a strange feeling even thinking of other's schedules for the first time in weeks, but not too strange that I didn't first grab the great breakfast spread on the way out.

I parked my bike leaning against a nearby wall, ready to attack the inclement elements, and I went to sit down in the breakfast room, dressed in full foul-weather gear from neck to bike shoes. I was layered with my Bike Mafia cycling hoodie, long cycling pants, long-sleeved jersey, fluorescent foul-weather jacket, gloves and shoe booties, ready to go.

The Wyndham did not hold back. No scraps left by the Kenosha Kickers like in Sheboygan. Eggs, bacon, pancakes, cereal, coffee and juices welcomed me as my shoes clip-clopped to the table.

Re-checking my route, my day looked to be only 52 miles, probably three-and-a half hours with the weather. I was not too worried. The first half of the ride was new to me, but the last half I had ridden hundreds of times. I knew each turn in my head.

Stuffed from breakfast, I walked once more through those automatic sliding doors, and into a deluge. It was torrential. If Noah had been faced with rain like this, he would have said, "Screw it!" and left with his ark one-quarter full. I had a schedule to keep. I was sure it would lighten up at some point.

Heading south, right away I got on another beautiful bike path, the Kenosha County Bike Trail. Even with the rain, it was lovely not to be dealing with car and truck spray and to just worry about those damn painted lines. I have skidded, and seen other riders get flattened, due to bike tire meeting the combination of painted road surface lines and rain.

The vision of past rides brought to the surface that one rainy day when a friend, eager to ride with our group but probably not as experienced, hit one of those lines and immediately went down. Hitting first with the front of his face, his cry of, "I think I ripped my lips off!" has never left me. He recovered, lips still intact, but it took a long while for him to rejoin the group. Being the last day of this journey, I was intent on keeping my lips in one piece as well.

The Kenosha path immediately turned into the Robert McClory Bike path at the Illinois state line. My heart sank when I saw the path, all 15 miles of it. The path was not the black-topped kind, like the Kenosha County that I anticipated, but was that dreaded crushed limestone. I have learned also there are different versions of crushed limestone. There is the terrible kind like I rode on and abandoned, after Petoskey. There is a well-maintained, super hard, good kind like the Devil River path outside Manitowoc.

This looked somewhere in between, and I was facing 15 miles of it in the rain. When you ride on limestone and it is not pressed hard, those little pieces fly up and cake everything, everywhere. You get chalky pieces in your mouth, your eyes, your shoes, up and down your back, down your neck, caking your brakes and your chain.

I had no alternative. I just had to slug through that temporary torture, my speed now down to 12 or 13 miles per hour. That one path alone would take me well over an hour.

Around Lake Bluff, I finally left the limestone behind and jumped on the North Shore Bike Path, heading west and then hoping to jog south again on the Skokie Valley Bike Path. That is where it got complicated. During the transition from McClory to the North Shore path, the rain really started picking up again, to the point that when I was in the middle of the North Shore, I had the recreation of the hard rain drops destroying my screen and trying to interpret Russian like when I was leaving Sleeping Bear on my way to Petoskey.

Couple that with the blinding, hard rain itself, the nearby wash coming off the cars immediately to my left, and the bad, in-need-of-repair popping-up bike path surface, and I blew right past my turn on to the Skokie path and kept going west. I ended up going a couple of miles out of my way until I just felt something was not as it should be. Able to check with "Karen" finally, and re-input English and my route, I saw the evils of my way, and had to backtrack and find the Skokie Path.

I had ridden on the Skokie and the next path, the North Branch Trail, many times. But being a city guy, that was as far I would go typically before heading home. The Skokie Path was a black-topped 11-mile straight shot, that transitioned, after some zigging and zagging through neighborhoods, to the north entry point of the North Branch Bike Path, named after the north branch of the Chicago River. This path, I had had the fortune to ride hundreds of times over a couple of decades, and I knew it like Jeanine's face, an old friend.

I sensed I was behind my time, as they say, but at this point I did not care. I had not budgeted for the 15 miles on crappy limestone, rain the entire way, or getting lost. All I wanted was to see Jeanine and the kids, a warm shower, and a cold beer. My thoughts shifted back to sights and sounds from days past. I thought about the lake itself. My trip took me more than 1,100 miles over 15 days. That is typically what the average commuter drives in their gas and electric-powered vehicles over a whole month. Fifteen days is your average worker's vacation not counting the third-time Grandma died and fake COVID-illness days.

If you walked along every foot of its shoreline it would be more than 1,400 miles. The lake is just huge, more than 300 miles north to south, 118 miles east to west at its widest, and three and a half miles where the Mackinac Bridge connects, at its narrowest.

My thoughts flashed back to days prior to the ride, sitting with friends when the conversation shifted to my ride. The story began about this person and that person who had had some cycling mishap. Some had ended up in the hospital; others choosing never to ride again.

I sat there, unusually quiet. It was not the negative spin that concerned me for I knew my friends meant no ill will. Instead, I was even more excited to start, yet knowing mindfulness was in order. I knew I had to be "in the moment" the whole trip around the lake. A few miles from the finish, mindful of my good fortune and amazing experiences, I felt a sense of accomplishment. I had been tested in every way possible, be it hills, wind, cold rain, bike issues or the long miles, and I had come out better for it. Instead of never wanting to get on a bike again I was thinking, "what's next?"

Images reappeared. Two random oversized T-Rexes, one in lower Michigan, the other in the UP, an oversized concrete Sasquatch jutting out from the forest and the creepy Harbor Motel pop into my head. The full-sized buck standing defiantly, and me not paying attention as I rode right over the dead porcupine.

The miles and miles of quiet road. The chilling rains. That dreaded limestone. The warm diners and their hearty fare. The "el Chapo" pickup transit across the Mackinac Bridge. The Guinness at St. Brendan's. The surprise at St. Brendan's. The world's largest hot dog. Little Johnny's interview interruption. I thought about the steep hills, one after the other, in northern Michigan, fighting each peddle push in my lowest gear, and then the joy of not having to pedal as I roared down the other side of those same hills.

The kind bike shop owners. My $9 Dollar General ear buds, still blasting away, despite the rain. The kind people I met everywhere.

I had seen the Midwest at speeds exceeding 40 miles per hour as I screamed down those Sleeping Bear hills, and as slow as 3 miles per hour at the steepest point standing on my pedals, and every gear in between.

Being on familiar ground, and knowing I was close, I picked up speed. As if it was finally saying, "I give up, you win," the rain softened to a mist as I finally left the path and cut through Chicago neighborhoods, first Edgebrook, then Jefferson Park. A mile from that cold beer, I zigzagged south, then west, then south again until I finally turned right on Erin and Joe's street, not sure what was next. I rolled up on to their front walk, and friends, family, strangers, even the FedEx guy with impeccable timing, emerged from the house and surrounded me, beer in their hands, smiles on their faces.

I heard a chorus of "You made it!" "Welcome home!" and "What took you so long?" simultaneously. I shrugged my shoulders as an answer to the last. I looked like I had just swam across Lake Michigan in full rain gear and felt the same. I was bushed. Straddling the Trek Terror, still showing caked limestone remnants from hours ago plastered on me and the bike, I was finally at rest. Grabbing the outstretched Modelo, I drank it in one long gulp. I was home. It was good to be home.

I may take tomorrow off.

Made in the USA
Monee, IL
02 July 2024

60822512R00095